A Second Blooming

Reading the essays in *A Second Blooming* I was immediately reminded of Winston Churchill's memorable appeal to the British people in 1941 in the darkest days of the German Blitzkrieg: "Never, never, never give up." Susan Cushman's anthology brings that message home to all readers, women and men, in a collection of powerful, lyrical, unforgettable prose.

— Lee Gutkind, editor of *Creative Nonfiction*

You will find yourself somewhere in Susan Cushman's *A Second Blooming*. I discovered pieces of me within these testimonies. The women in this book don't preach. There are no sermons. Turning their adversities into advantages, each one has lived to testify to the severe depths at which they traveled to get where they are. It's not an overstatement to say I loved this book. I didn't find instruction or admonishment but I did find a greater sense of comfort, familiarity, and empowerment. And God. He's present in every chapter. These inspirational stories breathe frost and fire, offering hope and second chances. Beautifully written and heartrending, *A Second Blooming* is a must read!

— Pamela King Cable, best-selling author of
The Sanctum, Southern Fried Women, and *Televenge*

A Second Blooming reads like an urgent prayer. Inside, courageous women writers relate painfully honest stories sure to inspire not only survival but thrive-al. Filled with heartbreaking transitions from past selves to new, it's a must read for any woman tattered by life and circumstances, eager to rise from the ashes again.

— Nicole Seitz, author of *The Cage-Maker,*
Trouble the Water, and *Saving Cicadas*

MERCER UNIVERSITY PRESS

Endowed by

TOM WATSON BROWN

and

THE WATSON-BROWN FOUNDATION, INC.

A Second Blooming

Becoming the Women We Are Meant to Be

Edited by Susan Cushman

MERCER UNIVERSITY PRESS | *Macon, Georgia*

2017

MUP/ P542

© 2017 by Mercer University Press
Published by Mercer University Press
1501 Mercer University Drive
Macon, Georgia 31207
All rights reserved

9 8 7 6 5 4 3 2 1

Books published by Mercer University Press are printed on acid-free paper that meets the requirements of the American National Standard for Information Sciences—Permanence of Paper for Printed Library Materials.

ISBN   978-0-88146-612-6
Cataloging-in-Publication Data is available from the Library of Congress

Contents

Foreword

Becoming the Person You Were Meant to Be: Where to Start*

Anne Lamott

We begin to find and become ourselves when we notice how we are already found, already truly, entirely, wildly, messily, marvelously who we were born to be. The only problem is that there is also so much other stuff, typically fixations with how people perceive us, how to get more of the things that we think will make us happy, and with keeping our weight down. So the real issue is how do we gently stop being who we aren't? How do we relieve ourselves of the false fronts of people-pleasing and affectation, the obsessive need for power and security, the backpack of old pain, and the psychic Spanx that keeps us smaller and contained?

Here's how I became myself: mess, failure, mistakes, disappointments, and extensive reading; limbo, indecision, setbacks, addiction, public embarrassment, and endless conversations with my best women friends; the loss of people without whom I could not live, the loss of pets that left me reeling, dizzying betrayals but much greater loyalty, and overall, choosing as my motto Wil-

---

liam Blake's line that we are here to learn to endure the beams of love.

Oh, yeah, and whenever I could, for as long as I could, I threw away the scales and the sugar.

When I was a young writer, I was talking to an old painter one day about how he came to paint his canvases. He said that he never knew what the completed picture would look like, but he could usually see one quadrant. So he'd make a stab at capturing what he saw on the canvas of his mind, and when it turned out not to be even remotely what he'd imagined, he'd paint it over with white. And each time he figured out what the painting wasn't, he was one step closer to finding out what it was.

You have to make mistakes to find out who you aren't. You take the action, and the insight follows: You don't think your way into becoming yourself.

I can't tell you what your next action will be, but mine involved a full stop. I had to stop living unconsciously; as if I had all the time in the world. The love and good and the wild and the peace and creation that are you *will* reveal themselves, but it is harder when they have to catch up to you in roadrunner mode. So one day I did stop. I began consciously to break the rules I learned in childhood: I wasted more time, as a radical act. I stared off into space more, into the middle distance, like a cat. This is when I have my best ideas, my deepest insights. I wasted more paper, printing out instead of reading things on the computer screen. (Then I sent off more small checks to the Sierra Club.)

Every single day I try to figure out something I no longer agree to do. You get to change your mind—your parents may have accidentally forgotten to mention this to you. I cross *one* thing off the list of projects I mean to get done that day. I don't know all that many things that are positively true, but I do know two things for sure: first of all, that no woman over the age of

forty should ever help anyone move, ever again, under any circumstances. You have helped enough. You can say no. No is a
complete sentence. Or you might say, "I can't help you move
because of certain promises I have made to myself, but I would
be glad to bring sandwiches and soda to everyone on your crew at
noon." Obviously, it is in many people's best interest for you not
to find yourself, but it only matters that it is in yours—and your
back's—and the whole world's, to proceed.

Acknowledgments

Almost every time I read a book I check out the acknowledgments, curious to find out if the author or editor received help from an agent, a publisher, early readers, writing groups, or family and friends. I am overflowing with gratitude to the people in those categories who helped me give birth to *A Second Blooming*.

I will mention my neighbor, Sally Palmer Thomason, and our mutual friend, Jennifer Bradner, in my introduction. As I was telling them both—over coffee at Sally's house just across the street from me—about my idea of putting together an anthology, they jumped in with suggestions. I'm not sure I would have undertaken this project without their strong encouragement.

Having contributed essays to three anthologies, I was anxious to try my hand at editing. The first people I asked for advice were Jennifer Horne and Wendy Reed. Jennifer and Wendy were co-editors of *Circling Faith: Southern Women on Spirituality*, the first anthology to publish one of my pieces. They were so patient with me as I bombarded them with e-mails for editorial advice. They recommended presses to query and gave feedback on the book proposal I created. Over a period of almost a year, they continued to answer questions and cheer me on as the project progressed.

The gracious people at Mercer University Press are a delight to work with. From his initial response to my query, Director Marc Jolley showed enthusiasm for the project, saying, "Even if you publish this elsewhere, I'm going to buy a copy for my wife!" Always patient with this newbie editor, he taught me valuable lessons in the art of publishing. Thanks also to his staff: Marsha Luttrell, Mary Beth Kosowski, Candice Morris, and Jenny Toole.

Finally, I am beyond humbled that twenty brilliant and generous authors agreed to entrust their work to my care. They all seemed to catch my excitement about the project and were happy to jump on board. All I can say is *thank you, thank you, thank you!* Would you like to meet them? Just turn the page…

Introduction

Susan Cushman

I have enjoyed greatly the second blooming that comes when you finish the life of the emotions and of personal relations and suddenly find—at the age of fifty, say—that a whole new life has opened before you, filled with things you can think about, study or read about.... It is as if a fresh sap of ideas and thoughts was rising in you. —Agatha Christie

This book was conceived in February 2015 over a cup of coffee at the kitchen table of my neighbor, Sally Palmer Thomason. Sally is an octogenarian and published author who has become a mentor to me. I had recently hosted a salon in my home at which Sally was the presenter. The salon topic was aging. We discussed Sally's book, *The Living Spirit of the Crone: Turning Aging Inside Out* (Fortress Press, 2006), which grew out of the doctoral dissertation she began when she was sixty-five. I was sixty-three when I moved in across the street from Sally, and my life began to change in a new and generative manner.

I say "generative" because that's what our lives should become if we devote the second half to individuation, as Carl Jung suggested. Sally defines it this way: "Individuation is a personal task to uncover the self that lies beneath and beyond the personal ego that has been formed through adaptation to culture." And, as Anne Lamott says, "The culture lies."

Having just read Richard Rohr's book *Falling Upward: A Spirituality For the Two Halves of Life*, I embraced his vision for cultural elders as heroes in our communities. A hero, as Rohr says, "is by definition a 'generative' person...concerned about the next generation and not just himself or herself.... The hero's journey is always an experience of an excess of life, a surplus of energy, with plenty left over for others." As a woman clearly trying to find my way through the second half of life, I wanted to be a generative person. I wanted to be a hero.

Maybe I've been on this path for a decade or more already. Surviving cancer at age fifty—the same year my youngest child left home for college—I read these words by the poet Mary Oliver: "Tell me, what is it you plan to do with your one wild and precious life?" I began following my creative desires more fully. I spent five or six years visiting monasteries and focusing on painting icons with egg tempera in the ancient Byzantine style. During and after that era I began writing nonfiction essays, attending workshops and conferences and submitting my work to various journals and magazines. As I learned more about both crafts, I yearned to share these skills with others, which I've done in the form of teaching iconography workshops and organizing and leading writing conferences and workshops. At some point I set for myself a goal of publishing a book by age sixty. I drafted four book-length manuscripts. The fourth is a novel, *Cherry Bomb*, which I hope has found a publishing home by the time this anthology comes out.

But sixty stretched to sixty-two the year I had a head-on collision with an ambulance. I was driving alone late one night on a country road outside Fairhope, Alabama, having just met with the editors and some of the other contributors to another anthology, *The Shoe Burnin': Stories of Southern Soul,* in preparation for a promotional trailer to be filmed the next day. I broke my neck, right leg, and ankle, and spent the next few days in a trauma center in Pensacola, Florida. Then came four months of sleeping in a hospital bed in my downstairs office, using a wheelchair, walker, and finally crutches, having more surgery, and undergoing lots of physical therapy. It was six months before I could remove the neck brace. It's amazing how physical trauma can cause brain fog. For nearly a year I couldn't work on the novel, but I gained so much more than I lost. I began to see with different eyes and to embrace the next season of my life with a clearer vision of myself and the world around me. I began to feel less like a flighty young woman and more like an elder.

The authors in this book aren't all elders. At least not chronologically. But all have in one way or another embraced the second half of their lives with a generative spirit. They have each had (or continue to have) a second blooming. As Rohr says, it's not about age: "When I say that you will enter the second half of life, I don't mean it in a strictly chronological way. Some young people, especially those who have learned from early suffering, are already there, and some older folks are still quite childish."

For example, thirty-two-year-old Nicole Marquez is way ahead of many of her chronological elders. This beautiful young dancer from Mississippi, pursuing her dream of Broadway, survived a fall from the roof of her five-story apartment building in New York City when she was twenty-five. Unwilling to give up her goal to dance, she now combines that gift with motivational speaking and acting. I've never met a more generative spirit. She would tell you she's become the next thing she's meant to be, but not without lots of help from her mother, Susan Marquez, her caregiver, who tells their story in "A Second Chance at Empty-Nesting."

Like Nicole, I was given a second chance, as were others in this anthology. Some of their lives were changed by trauma, some by incarceration, some by the loss of a loved one, some by marriages gone wrong or by new careers gone right.

A Second Blooming. These are stories of women of all ages who have made it over a "wall" to find their true selves. As Anne Lamott says in her essay—which we have used as a Foreword to the book—she escaped the "psychic Spanx that keeps us smaller and contained" and found herself by slowing down and living consciously.

In the first section, "Blooming through Surrender," we meet Suzanne Henley, whose work renovating Victorian homes and creating works of art reflects her journey through rehab for extreme anxiety and depression following her husband's years of drug abuse, all of which she explores in "Beyond this Point There Be Dragons." In "The Sweet Hereafter," the memoirist Mary Karr shares how surrendering can "bloom me more solidly into myself," after spending time in what she calls "the loony bin" and later with a group of women trying to stay sober.

Section two, "Blooming after Loss," opens with Kathy Rhodes's essay, "Pushing Up the Sun," in which she writes about the process of "unfolding" and following the cycles of nature after the death of her husband. In "Chapter 21" from Jessica Handler's memoir, *Invisible Sisters*, Jessica becomes the memory-keeper for her family after the deaths of both her sisters. Julie Cantrell considers her own blooming—and her brother's—nineteen years after his death by suicide in "My Brother's Keeper." NancyKay Sullivan Wessman writes about the magic of a marriage later in life, followed by the grief of loss and then open doors to a career as a writer when her "fifteen-year love affair" ends suddenly in "The Widow Wessman." River Jordan spins a tale of a dark, death-defying journey, resurrected life, and the miracle of new love in her lyric essay "Root."

The third section, "Blooming in Place," follows four authors on their adventures in Prague, Italy, Texas, and Kentucky. It starts with Nina Gaby—now an advanced practice psych nurse—who faces down her demon drink and several shady men in a small Italian town in "A Couple Bad Nights in Brindisi." Forty-two-year-old Beth Ann Fennelly returns to Prague two decades after her first visit to Silesia in "When Dusk Fell an Hour Earlier," but with a very different memory of how things had played out. Had Prague had a second blooming, or was it her own maturity that gave her a new outlook on earlier events? Alexis Paige weaves two stories—one of her sexual assault in Italy and the other of her incarceration for drunk driving in Texas—through her gut-wrenching essay, "Syringa Vulgaris," which also involves depression, suicide attempts, and substance abuse, and finally finds her at home with her husband in a serene setting in New England. And finally, in the third edition of Kim Michele Richardson's memoir about the abuse she suffered in a Catholic orphanage in Kentucky, *The Unbreakable Child*, she writes a scathing letter to the Vatican. Blessed to have what she calls second, third, and fourth chapters to her life, she offers forgiveness while calling the clergy to accountability in "Abuse: A Survivor's Message for the Vatican."

"Blooming Again…and Again," the fourth section, contains five essays, starting with Wendy Reed's "Woman on a Half Shell," in which she explores themes of feminism, intimacy in marriage, and the power of "women of a certain age," even making a pilgrimage to the Fountain of Youth in St. Augustine, Florida, with her sisters. Fifty-something (and slim and fit) Ellen Morris Prewitt reflects on second chances and life before and after having both hips replaced in "The Walker." Freelance writer Susan Marquez is given "A Second Chance at Empty Nesting" following years of caregiving for her daughter, who fell from the roof of her five-floor apartment building in New York City. Sally Palmer Thomason—an octogenarian who acknowledges that her "second blooming" happened in her sixties—explains how the wisdom of ancient traditions gives insight into the stages of life in "The Triskele." And finally, after being on her own at fifteen, Jennifer Bradner shares her story of healing from abandonment, burning through the karma she created for herself, and moving into midlife with a clear mind in "Dharma Slut."

The last section features four authors writing about "Blooming in Careers and Communities." Cassandra King candidly describes the death to her old self and her blooming in a new marriage and career as a writer in "Something Has to Die." In "My Eudaimonia," Emma French Connolly, a former parish deacon in an Episcopal church in Memphis, begins to discover her true self as she opens a needle and craftworks shop on Magazine Street in New Orleans in her seventh decade. The poet and author Jennifer Horne seeks "a more dangerous centrality" in the second half of her life, motivated—by her mother's poetry and resilience—to put art first, as she explains in "The Second Half." Former poet laureate of the United States, Natasha Trethewey, writes about the importance of uniting communities around collective and personal memories in "Liturgy," an excerpt from her book *Beyond Katrina: A Meditation on the Mississippi Gulf Coast*.

In whatever decade of our lives it happens, we all eventually hope to emerge from the chrysalis we built for our younger selves and transform into the beautiful women we are meant to be. This transformation—this blooming—doesn't happen organically, without the application of a tremendous amount of creative energy and action on our part. As E. E. Cummings said, "It takes courage to grow up and become who you really are."

I

Blooming through Surrender

෨

In the loony bin, I surrendered—not full bore, the way saints do, once and for all, blowing away my ego in perfect service to God—not even close…. Before, I'd feared surrender would sand me down to nothing. Now I've started believing it can bloom me more solidly into myself.

—Mary Karr
(from "The Sweet Hereafter" in *Lit*)

Beyond this Point There Be Dragons

Suzanne Henley

Unexplored areas of medieval world maps were illustrated with drawings of vicious, fire-spitting dragons, often with the warning "Beyond this Point There Be Dragons."

The curtains are drawn, the room only dimly lit from the outside hall, the shadows darkening against the winter afternoon. Frightened, I lie on my left side in sheets limp from my sweat, as my right leg rises, involuntary and jerky, and then slams back down against my left thigh and ankle. Over and over. I cannot stand, only lie and watch as though in a different, observant body. I lie crumpled, exhausted, sweaty, and riveted by confusion at this side effect of the pharmacy pumping through my body.

Silence eats at the deepening shadows, the only sound my right leg scuffing the jeans of my left leg as it jerks and falls from its ratcheted height. I did not know a body could have commands separate from the me I knew.

I lie curled in the dark, suckling my demons.

᠅

"Well, I think it's time we nipped this in the bud," my psychologist Kip said. I had paged him from my kitchen, where, without warning as I wrote a grocery list for a dinner party I was hosting two nights later, a panic attack began.

I had taught school while my husband was a graduate school student in English. He decided he wanted to become a doctor, however, and taught college English while taking undergraduate science courses to prepare for his medical school application. I continued teaching as he went through medical school, fulfilled the intense year of internship, and switched specialties halfway through residency training. These were difficult years. We had three children—all beautiful in many ways—and owed thousands of dollars in loans. Both our workloads were heavy, and, whenever he managed to come home, he was met by a tired wife and the demands of three young children. I told myself, "Things will get better after..., things will get better after..., things will get better after...."

But they didn't.

In a three-day period, three weeks after he began his first position with a large medical group after ten years of preparation, our world, already teetering, slid into chaos. Alarmed by his increasingly bizarre behavior, one day I went upstairs to his study, looking around randomly, and popped open his black medical bag. It took a few moments for the significance of its contents to register: a handful of syringes, gauze tourniquets, and vial after vial of some unknown liquid labeled "Fentanyl." I did not know what it was and called a hospital pharmacy to ask. "Ma'am, it's the most powerful narcotic made. It's forty to fifty times stronger than heroin. You can't get a prescription; only hospitals have it. You have to steal it. If you know someone taking this stuff, call the police. 'Cause the person will be dead soon."

I hung up the phone as the pieces of my life slowly spun and fell around me in ripped-out edges onto the kitchen floor.

That evening my husband drove home in an unexpected new car, a convertible. We went to a dinner party with his new medical group. All evening I sat terrified with my knowledge as I tried to make conversation with the newly met wives. When we got home, I told him what I'd discovered that morning. Quietly, for hours, I talked and he raged and denied until, suddenly, right before the sun came up, he admitted everything. He said he knew he'd reached tolerance and was waiting to either die or be arrested.

He called Lakeside Hospital and was told he had to come in for twenty-eight days. He said he couldn't, he'd be fired. He was told withdrawal would take twenty-four hours and to start going to AA.

That day and night were like a low-budget movie, a grainy parody of drug withdrawal, but it was of course only too real. I wept in horror and helplessness at his anguish. The next morning he called Lakeside again and was told that before coming in he first had to tell his medical group what he'd been doing.

He was fired immediately. I drove him to Lakeside and went to tell my parents what had happened. A new way of life had begun.

During the next two years there were more jobs, more firings, more rehabs. One night—after being fired for having shot up during surgery with a drug he mistook for Fentanyl but instead was a drug used to suppress the lungs—he came home and, without speaking, went into the bathroom. I could hear what I recognized as the sound of bullets being spun and clicking in a revolver. I hadn't even known he had a gun. I picked up my two youngest, one in each arm, just as he came out of the bathroom. I stood paralyzed, saw the bulge of the gun in his pocket, and knew I could not move fast enough holding the two children. He asked me to take a walk with him. In a quick exchange, not knowing if he also meant to kill me outside where the children could not see, I somehow persuaded him that he needed to go take a drive alone. He left. I heard his car drive away and, shaking with a mixture of anger and fear, called his AA friend, who asked me, "Don't you know he just needs to be mothered?"

My fury was lined with granite. The medical board sent him out of town to a four-month rehab.

Shortly after he returned, my father died. Until that first night sitting with my mother in the family home, I had accepted my marriage as my responsibility, a promise I'd made, a given in my life in the same way that I had naturally curly hair and wore a size nine shoe.

If you're told every day you didn't mop the kitchen floor the right way, however, you look up finally one morning and realize you've been mopping that floor every day for fourteen years trying, unaware, to save a man from himself and that, day by day, over and over, a molecule of your soul has lost its breath. I went home and told my husband I wanted a divorce.

We began seeing Kip, a psychologist recommended by many, for counseling because my husband asked me to go. Ironically, I'd been asking that we go for years; he'd always refused. Now, however, even knowing the impact a divorce would have on our three young children, I was past caring, but I reluctantly agreed to go.

In my ignorance and haughtiness I dismissed Kip, too. He was too young—he looked as though he'd just walked off a high school baseball diamond; his accent was too Southern; he wore the wrong kind of shoes. He could not possibly have anything worth saying to me.

The panic attacks, which had begun two months earlier without warning, increased. At the time, little was known about them. They were often accompanied by a rush to a hospital with a diagnosis of stroke or heart attack. My first attack happened in a grocery checkout line. Gripping my cart's handle, I became gradually and frighteningly aware that I couldn't breathe. My arms and legs felt as though they were disembodied, and I was convinced I was becoming irretrievably crazy, about to be flung as jagged shrapnel to circle in orbit, trapped, for oblivion. My heart, as though on a loud speaker, skipped beats and pounded in my ears, filling my head with enormous pressure. Convinced I was having a heart attack or stroke, I gasped in heaves, grasping for air.

I had no frame of reference for this experience. When you scrape your knee, when you hit your elbow—or even break a bone—you know the level of pain to expect. And when it's over, it's over. The reality of a full-blown anxiety attack hits you without warning, however; the fear does not recede but increases. The dread of recurring attacks is substantial and terrifying. You don't know you're having one until, too late, it is already occurring. Time slows, the landscape reels. The fear smells like a feral animal.

Over the next few weeks, wherever I happened to be when an attack occurred became off-limits. The fear of a recurrence—at any one of an increasing number of stores or in an elevator—quickly shrank what some internal, primitive animal antennae marked as the perimeter of my safe universe. I, who only a few years earlier had hitchhiked through seven European countries and, without a second thought, through the Alps in the middle of a blizzard in a truck hauling sheep, could now not imagine driving across a short, nondescript city bridge. My house was the one place I felt safe, the one haven I knew I could count on.

And now it had happened. In my safe space. Standing in my kitchen, I shook trying to dial Kip's pager number. When it beeped, I slammed my phone number into his pager.

"Yep, we need to nip this in the bud," Kip repeated. "Meet me at the hospital and we'll take care of this."

Watching my three-year-old and four-year-old playing on the kitchen floor, I thought, "Oh, shit, yes, thank Jesus. I'll be in a bed resting on flowered sheets like the ones in the maternity ward while caring, knowledgeable nurses take care of me. I can order special meals brought to my bed while something magic erases this nightmare from my life. And then—yes!—I'll be home in two days and can still have the dinner party."

"Where do I meet you, Kip?"

"Oh, just in the lobby. I'll get out there as soon as I can."

"'Out there'? Where exactly is 'out there'?" I asked, confused. I'd thought he meant downtown at Baptist Hospital, where I'd had my three children and there were flowered sheets.

"Lakeside. The lobby at Lakeside," he said.

My stomach clinched. "Lakeside?!" my head screamed, Lakeside, where my husband had gone for his first drug rehab three years earlier, the month that publicly marked the beginning of the long, frayed end of my marriage? And now Kip was calmly telling me I would be going to that other unit, the psych unit at the opposite end of the building that I had scorned back then as a scapegoat. My husband was a doctor with a drug habit, yes, but those people were all crazy, I thought in my warped reasoning. From my vantage point then, that unit at the other end of the hall full of lost, shuffling, crazy souls had meant that we were not at the bottom of the barrel. *They* were.

And now *I* was.

My envisioned weekend on flowered sheets became not a weekend but eight and one-half weeks. My sheets were limp with sweat. There were no flowers.

⁓

After talking to Kip, I packed an overnight bag. My eleven-year-old daughter came home from school, my mother picked up my three children, and my friend Patti drove me to the hospital on its mockingly pastoral acres in the countryside. Making jokes and cackling with *M*A*S*H*-like humor, we stopped on the way for carryout coffee as though we were on a winter road trip to the beach.

As promised, Kip met me in the lobby and introduced me to my psychiatrist, who would evaluate my condition and prescribe medication. Barbara Chamberlin was under five feet tall and looked like a porcelain doll with her smooth skin, large, bright eyes, and glistening teeth. Disheveled, I was exhausted from the attack's aftermath and the massive adrenalin rush of the afternoon. I knew how to meet and chat with people at parties, how to initiate and lead classroom discussions. I had no clue, however, how to negotiate a conversation in a psychiatric hospital lobby. This was not a cocktail party.

We walked down the hall and through a heavy industrial door that closed with a commanding swoosh, an echoing click as it locked. I was left at the nurses' station with my overnight bag.

"This here's all you brought?" the plus-sized nurse in blue scrubs asked as she opened my bag and started emptying each item onto the counter.

"Uh, yeah, just for the weekend," I said, breathing lightly.

Her eyebrows rose, lips tightened.

"Well, you can't have this," she snorted, lifting my razor out of the bag and plunking it against the Formica counter. "Or these!" she said, holding up a small glass bottle of perfume—twirling it to read the label—and a narrow crocodile belt I wore with my jeans.

"But why not?" I was growing alarmed.

"Because you might try to slit your wrists or your neck or hang yourself. We gotta protect you from yourself!" And she scooped the rest of the items back into my suitcase and snapped the locks with finality. "Here you go, honey. It's yours now," she said, sliding my suitcase across the counter toward me. Her nails were bitten off at the quick.

I can still remember this moment and the snap of the suitcase locks. I knew I was in a psychiatric unit and I had heard the hissing pneumatic lock of the door echoing down the concrete-block hallway, but not until that moment did I feel the icy frisson of hairs standing up across the back of my neck like those of a trapped animal. As an aide walked me down a long, shadowed hallway to show me to my room, I remembered the inscription over Dante's gate to hell: "Abandon hope, all ye who enter here."

That night the demons I'd controlled for so many years unleashed themselves, a tsunami of depression and despair and panic. The attacks came one after another. A nurse sat across from my bed, leaning toward me from a chair, and held my hands. She looked unwavering into my eyes, which darted in terror, and told me quietly and evenly to breathe deeply and slowly. She gave me a shot. As I drifted to sleep in the anonymous, institutional room under the cheap, thin bedspread, I said good-bye to the world I'd known for forty years.

I became a guinea pig. Because my reaction to any therapeutic drugs was an unknown, a hit-and-miss barrage of different medications exploded in my body. I was simultaneously exhausted and wired. Nothing worked. My blood pressure zoomed out of control. I remember the horrified look on the doctor's face as I tried at one point to describe the fluorescent orange spikes that registered like a vivid EKG printout across my mind's eye when I spoke. Trying to see through the glaring, frantic static while talking was frustrating. I reached forward, attempting to touch the fluorescent spikes, but the moving image was not external—only in my head. The doctor left the room abruptly, a fixed expression on her face, and came back quickly, armed with an unnamed pill.

I could not control my legs easily and had to lean against the wall for support and balance as I walked down the hall. Likewise, whenever I had a phone call on the communal wall phone, I lacked the energy to stand up straight, and the phone cord was not long enough to reach the floor, so I had to hug the wall with the phone propped against my shoulder. Conversations were tiring and nonsensical. Words seemed to jerk out of my mouth.

I was literally locked into this unit. Other patients could sign out to go outside during the day, but for my first two weeks I was not allowed to leave the unit. And I didn't want to leave. I didn't look out of windows; even the distant, faint sound of trucks rushing along a nearby expressway filled me with un-grounded dread. The minutiae of the normal, commonplace world was too threatening. I stayed exhausted from hair-trigger responses to the insignificant. Even the shower was threatening and claustrophobic.

Meals were a problem. Walking down the cafeteria line was like passing through a gauntlet. The food repulsed me; the smell of heated industrial plastic trays and worn plastic plates, still damp from the dishwasher, was nauseating. I sat at random ta-bles simply staring at my tray. Peoples' conversations made no sense, and everyone seemed to talk in jarring, loud voices. The lighting was too harsh. People rising from their chairs loomed out of perspective and startled me. Although known to cuss as imaginatively as any sailor, I found the sound of any shouted cuss word offensive, physically abrasive.

I began to lose weight rapidly.

After weeks of becoming progressively sicker, all I knew was that, very simply, I wanted to die. I don't know which carried more lethal weight: the social and personal stigma of being in a psychiatric hospital, my inability to accept my vulnerability and loss of self, the various pills' side effects, or my resistance to let-ting them work.

I had failed. I was not worthy of getting well.

Daily group therapy was a requisite. I condescended. My re-sistance to the ideas of needing help and of help coming from the group process was formidable. These people I sat around in a circle with every day were not, I believed, acceptable. They were not my people. A tight, smug me thought I was better than they were: I had studied and traveled in Europe for two years, I had been chairman of an English department and instructor at two community colleges, I had just illustrated and written a cookbook. I knew "important" people in the city. I clung desperately to these illegitimate values.

I had always enjoyed analyzing and critiquing problems; I lived in my head, so I was comfortable telling the therapy group members what was wrong with each of them. It was not all right, however, for anyone to call me out. I would sit in tight, puffed-up anger thinking the stupid session was paying for one more tire on Kip's Porsche.

An unexpected betrayal were the cold, dismissive looks I got from my husband's AA friends I'd see down the hall visiting their friends in the alcohol and drug unit. Later I learned they'd told my husband that my going to Lakeside was my manipulation to coerce him to stay married. This was a double betrayal that cut to the bone.

My eight and a half weeks were punctuated, however, with moments of kindness and occasional humor. A couple of days after arriving, I walked into my room, and sitting on the chest of drawers in the dreary January light was an immense arrangement of spring flowers sent by my friend Barbara. Its colors—and the thought that she would treat my hospitalization like any other hospitalization, for a broken leg or childbirth—ripped through my shroud of stigma like momentary sunshine. I sat on my bed and wept. They were the only flowers I received in over eight weeks. I even wonder today, many "enlightened" years later, how many people send flowers to friends in a psychiatric unit.

My aunt and uncle, Sis and Ed, who lived in the country outside a small Southern town, called me most nights after early dinner, chatting nonchalantly, just to "check in," telling me each night, "It's all right, honey, you're going to be just fine, just fine." Although standing at the phone and carrying on a conversation took such effort, my gratitude at their easy conversation and reassurance continues to be one of my more important life lessons: Even if you don't send flowers, do show up. Just show up. And the words don't matter.

About a month after my admission, my friend Carol Ann took me out to dinner, my first trip out into the normal world. The night was dark and cold, the restaurant claustrophobic. On the way home she turned onto the wrong side of the dark divided highway going the wrong direction. We laugh about it now, but at the time it was a terrifying experience. A panic attack consumed me until I felt safe back at the hospital.

My friend Betsy also checked me out for a lunch trip to legendary Bozo's BBQ; Blanche, Robbie, and Janie visited once, uncertainty and concern marking their grouped faces as they walked down the long hall, the bag of coral knitting yarn they clutched a welcomed offering. Nina and Stan took my two youngest into their home, wrapping them in attention and security; Madge and Mary Linda made supportive visits throughout my hospitalization. My mother, my main ballast, defined the concept of unconditional love.

I was discharged after five and a half weeks without effective medication, and my depression quickly spread and flooded, a river breaching a levee. I have little memory of how the children got to school or how I prepared meals. I only remember the increasing thoughts of suicide as the sole remedy for the emotional and physical pain stalking my hours.

My depression was not just an emotional, mental pain; it pinned me to the bed, exhausted and withering. Writhing, black, prehistoric lizards from a tarry pit—scaly tongues flicking and wrapping around my lungs, dirty claws digging into my ribs— gorged on my heart and stomach, circling for the best attack, leaving flayed ends of jagged flesh as they consumed me from the inside out. I lay in bed sapped, paralyzed by their weight, sorting through different ways of killing myself. Driving off the bridge at full speed became my choice. A far-off flicker of reason registered feebly that I was dangerously sick when I knew I didn't care what my death would do to my three-, four-, and eleven-year-old children.

Ethel, who had worked with my family for almost thirty years, alternated with my mother in helping with the children. She came one morning, realized my condition, and called my mother, who came and drove me to the doctor's office. I was not allowed to leave the office, my mother was sent back to my house to pack a bag, and I was driven back to the hospital, where I was put on suicide watch, a burly aide planted in a chair in the doorway of my room.

I was forced again to go to group therapy, where I sat silent and motionless, the weight of depression squeezing and shriveling my breath. The third day the therapist suddenly stopped and made me get on the floor. I was made to crawl to each person's chair, stopping in front of each one in the circle and saying one reason not to kill myself.

The humiliation was intense.

But I was also stunned by the paradox that in humbling myself, kneeling prostrate before each of these once-dismissed fellow patients, I was in fact crawling toward healing. It was an epiphany, and I think I caught a glimpse of Jesus outside the door giving a high-five to a passing aide.

I have since learned that my recognition of truth most often occurs after the fact. I learn from seeing the backside of God, as we are reminded in Exodus when Yahweh and Moses have a little chat. I have come to know that humiliation often is the beginning of humility. And gratitude.

Coincidentally, and luckily, the doctor tried one more anti-depressant, a rarely used MAOI inhibitor carrying food prohibitions that, if not followed, can cause stroke or death. It slowly began to work. I felt like a swimmer held under canyons of deep, dark water too long slowly being pulled to the surface, light, and air. I gasped at new life.

I made one friend among the other patients. Bob and I had arrived at the hospital in the same week, with the same diagnosis of major anxiety and depression. We both were discharged after five and a half weeks, at home with no communication with each other for three weeks, and, in a surprise to both of us and a frowning concern of the staff, reentered the hospital within a day of each other. We both stayed for three more weeks.

Although we hadn't known each other before, we had mutual friends and acquaintances and shared the same off-the-wall sense of humor. We managed to turn the terrifying panic attacks we each had into a source of humor, sweat running down our faces and marking underarm rings on our shirts. We hunkered against the wall smoking and tried to one-up each other with the worst panic stories, and we used each other to measure our depths of depression. Also, he wore the right kind of shoes.

In our new worlds of healing, we became quite preadolescent. We played practical jokes on some of the other patients— we short-sheeted like master summer campers—and, because I told him about my fear of the psychiatric patients who had wandered the halls when I had visited my husband in the drug unit, we would purposely stagger around and act like caricatures of "crazy" patients during the other unit's visiting hours. Like twelve-year-olds, we laughed ourselves silly, shameless, at our cruel antics. Although no romantic feelings stirred in our relationship, during the last three weeks the staff reassigned me to a different therapy group to split us up. We had disrupted the whole unit.

As embarrassing as it is to think of our actions, they were, I believe, our way of combating depression, keeping that animal caged, taming it, a positive sign that each of us was helping the other heal. As our new medications began to work and I was allowed outside during the first warm days of spring, Bob and I would rush outside to the sun and lie on the hill by the lake in the new shoots of green grass, blowing smoke rings toward the sun. It was like being born again. We were weeds forcing through the cracks in concrete, cracks that we know metaphorically are where and how the light gets in, weeds ragged but green and reaching for the sun.

Bob and I haven't seen each other since and probably would not know how to greet each other in this world outside the life of the hospital, but he was a bit of magic sent to ease my passage through hell.

∼

Although I was far from healed, it was time to go home. Kip knew better than I the long road that lay ahead for me. His last words before I left the hospital were stunning: "We've tried every medication available, Suzanne. There isn't anything left—except to give God a chance." I found it startling to hear a psychologist give blatant theological advice. I had no idea who "God" was— certainly there had been no burning bushes or voices from a cloud during all this time, and praying was not a concept I understood or entertained. Years earlier I had ignorantly told my friend John, who'd invited my husband and me to his church, that I couldn't possibly go, that I would feel like a hypocrite unless I had a Saul-on-the-road-to-Damascus experience. He quietly replied, "But that's what the Episcopal Church does, Suzanne. It takes you wherever you are."

I remembered John's words after Kip discharged me and, without any thought of expectation or meaning or belief, began taking my three children to church.

I also had to see Kip for follow-up sessions for eight weeks after leaving the hospital. It was still difficult for me to drive far from home—spitting dragons continued to patrol the expressway lying in wait for me—but I made it each week. During one session I asked him why, weeks earlier during my inpatient stay, my patient notebook containing all the professional notes about me had disappeared from the nurses' station. I had asked the nurse where it was so I could sign out to walk to the lake. "They're discussing you in staff meeting," the nurse had said curtly. I had been furious at what I thought was the violation of my privacy. And now I was curious to hear Kip's response.

"Well," he said, clearing his throat, "you were the most depressed patient I'd ever treated." He paused, gauging my reaction, and looked me in the eye. "We didn't think you were going to make it."

And then, after a short silence, we both smiled.

❦

Slowly, over many months during which I continued to feel like an outcast, a social misfit, unable to concentrate or read or even put together two meaningful sentences, I gradually identified confidence in a new self.

Rehab is never speedy or cheap, whether one is talking about alcohol, drugs, psychiatry, hip replacement, or houses. The process is never a straight line; sacrifice is a given. Surprises and expense—whether emotional or for construction materials and labor—are guaranteed. It is physically exhausting and demonstrably rewarding. I enjoy the irony that, of the several different occupations I have had since leaving the hospital and returning to the world, one of the more fulfilling has been as a contractor rehabbing derelict, early twentieth-century cottages. I buy, gut, redesign, and renovate homes worn down by age and misuse, retaining the good bones and architectural integrity while reconstructing the living space. My crew, who over the years have become my second family, and I work hard creating new life, just as in the hospital I learned the necessities of rehabbing parts of myself, throwing out the dead and useless—as difficult as some of those rotting boards are to pull out, nail by nail—admiring the grain of old wood worth saving, and always checking the beams and foundation before tearing out a wall.

And, as trite as it is to say, we are all of course rehabs. Every moment. Every day. Even when we seem to be stuck out in some endless, parched desert, our hearts and souls cracking and dying of thirst, we're handed the gift of starting over. Failure simply means an opportunity to begin again. We get to wrench out those old, rusted nails we worked so hard to hammer in crooked-ly, pull out the warped boards, and try once more to hammer a straighter nail. Every day.

For thirty years I was a committed single working mother. My experiences had left me marriage-shy and feeling inept at relationships. Rearing three children and putting bread—meager slices—on the table, working hard at meaningful jobs, develop-ing rich friendships, and, most important, discovering myself filled my life. A few years ago, however, on the cusp of my eighth decade, I said "yes" to Jim, an extraordinary man of many dimensions, deeply wise and relentlessly funny, all edges lined in kindness. And it doesn't matter—almost—what kind of shoes he wears.

I no longer hitch rides through Alpine blizzards; my jour-neys now are usually internal, marked by detour signs, green lights, and amazement. I still occasionally spot dragons silhou-etted against the horizon of the expressway, but most are tooth-less and tired-looking, fires spent. They remind me, though, of Joan Didion's advice

> to keep on nodding terms with the people we used to be, whether we find them attractive company or not. Other-wise they turn up unannounced and surprise us, come

hammering on the mind's door at 4 a.m. of a bad night and demand to know who deserted them, who betrayed them, who is going to make amends.

So now I swaddle and cradle all those selves I used to be—many still spitting a need for control, willful, stubborn, scratching and muddied, scraping up the mined hillside of ignorance—and tote them over my shoulder stuffed in a patched and threadbare bag. They're still noisy and unruly but now fairly light baggage and, shifting their weight, I sing, slightly off-key, to them all, "Yes, thank you, thank you, yes!"

There are no regrets.

Gratitude is all.

Oh, yes.

The Sweet Hereafter

Mary Karr
from Lit

I am welcomed on a boat—it's a canoe hollowed from a dark tree. The canoe is incredibly wobbly, even when you sit on your heels. A balancing act. If you have the heart on the left side you have to lean a bit to the right, nothing in the pockets, no big arm movements, please, all rhetoric has to be left behind. Precisely: rhetoric is impossible here. The canoe glides out over the water.

—Tomas Tranströmer, "Standing Up"
(trans. Robert Bly)

In the loony bin, I surrendered—not full bore, the way saints do, once and for all, blowing away my ego in perfect service to God—not even close. But watching the world through chicken wire convinced me that my unguided thought process would no doubt swerve me into concrete. Before, I'd feared surrender would sand me down to nothing. Now I've started believing it can bloom me more solidly into myself.

So once home, I take suggestions I'd carped about before with a new zeal, albeit with the occasional snotty look on my face. I sit squirmy in prayer while conflicting thoughts zip through my skull like so many simultaneously slammed tennis balls. Before, prayer had involved bouncing on and off my knees so fast it resembled a break-dance move.

Make a daily gratitude list, Joan said, using every letter of the alphabet to delineate what you're grateful for.

Like *J* for Joan the Bone.

Bingo, she says.

You're not serious. That's so puerile.

Childish things for stubborn children, she says.

I'm teaching again with some ease, and the writing started in the hospital plows forward.

Warren and I exist like kindly intentioned siblings, though he's putting forth more effort. On my birthday, he stuns me by gathering friends at a restaurant to holler *surprise*, but when he reaches for me the next morning, I roll away. The prospect scares me. Never, I think, could I kiss that handsome mouth. Whatever his reaction stays shut inside him. I follow the old advice of St. Jack of the Tinfoil, who'd counseled me to fulfill my contract unless otherwise guided.

Right before I hit a year sober, Joan suggests starting a women's group for gab of some spiritual variety—think quilting bee where we stitch on each other's souls, autopsy where the corpses take turns carving. In my office at Radcliffe on Sunday nights, we meet—about four or five sober women trying to stay that way.

Nobody operates from a formal religious construct, no church ladies or temple mavens. Joan rustles up a list of discussion topics she used in a similar group, and we start off talking about prayer. When Deb claims her regular prayer is for a joyous day filled with serenity, I say, You can ask for that?

Nights I put Dev to bed, the St. Francis prayer becomes part of our ritual, in the form of call and response. I say, *Where there is hatred, let me sow*, and he shouts out, *Love*. I say, *Where there is conflict*, and he hollers, *Pardon*. Afterward, if I have trouble sleeping, I lie in a hot bath with a washcloth over my face, saying prayers I hardly believe but take blind comfort from.

I'm still given to cussing any traditional notion of God.

What god would deny you children? I say to Deb, for she's enduring torturous in vitro hormones trying to conceive. Some afternoons at the house, I inflict the agonizing shots, the big needle stiff in her muscle, while in the next room, a house resident may have popped out a second or third addicted or HIV-positive baby. Deb's calm baffles me.

I've let go, she says.

If you've surrendered, I say (I get maniacal in these arguments), wouldn't you stop using the hormones and harvesting the ova?

Deb says, It may not be right for me to conceive. But to pursue them and not get them will somehow turn out in my favor in some way I can't foresee now. (Years later Deb will divorce, and her ex will kill himself, and she'll tell me, *Now I see maybe why we could never get pregnant.*) I tell the other women that Deb doesn't even mark on her calendar when her period's due. Her doctor does that. She needs to relinquish all control.

Joan wonders if the rest of us could manage such faith, and we strike a deal that we'll all let go our own wills as openhandedly. In fact, until each of us has given up care of her life to some greater force for good, the group won't go on.

But I quibble so much about arcane definitions of *will* and *care* that the women wind up voting that I've surrendered already and am just being a bitch about it.

And to their will, I yield, which is a start.

With the group, I finally succumb to Joan's long-running nag that I list stuff I feel most crappy about—every single grudge and humiliation—a private exercise we all talk about over a month or so. I break mine into columns with the crappy thing on the left, the particular way it hurts me in the middle, my part in it on the right. In some cases—being sexually assaulted, say—my part has been burying or ignoring the awful event in a way that restabs the wound. Almost eighty pages, mine gets to be. Theirs are way shorter, since they've done this before.

Sitting in my posh office in low lamplight one Sunday, we unscrew Oreos and sip muddy coffee while privately rolling down our individual columns—we cherrypick what to share—and it floors me to see laid out how fear has governed pretty much my every moronic choice. I've never regarded myself as a fearful individual. I've hitchhiked in Mexico and blustered drunk into biker bars all mouthy. Those acts now strike me as more pitiful than brave—the sad bravado of a girl with little to lose.

We're supposed to go over the full grudge lists with another person, and Joan gives me a list of sober preachers and rabbis and priests who'll listen. In my shame, I half expect a religious guy to hurl lightning bolts down on my head.

A man with a thick Irish lilt answers one call. Come on over, he says. But would you mind bringing me a Coca-Cola? I crave the stuff and can't afford it.

I wind up in a room facing a guy in a monk's robe, a giant crucifix hanging from his belt like a scalp. Brother Francis (not his name) is over eighty and skeletally thin, with sunken cheeks and blue veins all over an age-spotted skull. The liter of Coke sits on the low table between us, alongside an ashtray. The instant I sit down, he pulls out a pack of rolling papers and constructs an immaculate ciggie while I light up. Both of us smoke like tar kilns the whole time as legal pads I flip through quickly pile in my lap—minor offenses. But when it comes to the wreckage of my romantic past, I stall, holding my Styrofoam cup as I press my thumbnail around the rim in a series of half moons.

We seem to have reached an impasse, he says.

Well, Francis, there are some things I'm uncomfortable talking about with you.

His thin lips draw on his hand-rolled stogie. He says with an expression of terrifying hilarity, Are they things of a *sexual* nature?

I nod.

He exhales smoke and says, Maybe I can put you at ease, for I've had more experience in that area than my vows would suggest.

He tells me some pretty hair-raising stories about his life in South America, when he was still on the whiskey. How he wound up joining a twelve-step program for people whose sexual natures were—in his words—severely disordered. His tale doesn't involve pedophilia or some fetish for disemboweling kittens or anything gross. But my betrayals—cheating on a college beau, making out with my English boyfriend's Afghan squash-playing pal—pretty much pale alongside his. I sit and listen until dark comes, and the next morning I come back for most of the day.

At the end, jazzed to the gills on many plastic bottles of Coke, I sit drained over the overflowing ashtray, and Brother Francis blinks behind his smeary horn-rims, saying, Leave all that stuff here with me. God wants you to put this stuff down now. Go wear the world like a loose garment. And be of good cheer. If you let God in, He'll take this shame from you.

Descending the subway stairs, I no longer ooze the sweaty, reptilian stench I walked in with, but I can't say I feel like I've wholly shed my past. That night, though, I sleep like somebody clocked with a sledgehammer. The next morning in the bathroom mirror, there's more shine in my eyes. Throughout the day, when my head lurches for the old miseries to start gnawing on, I have a touchstone phrase—*That's* done—I blurt internally as often as need be. The mind, whirring for decades at thousands of rpm's per second, keeps trying to fill in new freefalls of quiet. For the first time in my life, I got to sleep every night soundly, without medication, sometimes nine hours a pop.

Don't get me wrong. The irritation that once drove me like a cat-o'-nine-tails can start flailing in an instant. But now the car door I slam or the snipe I let fly at Warren trails an apology. I blurt out *sorry* nonstop, since I never again want to nurse such bitterness as I'd stored up before.

Once, I'm laden with parcels and carrying Dev up slick stairs on my hip after he's hurt his ankle, and he calls me *poopy head* so many times that I'm ready to fling him down and swear. But a quick prayer—*Please let me be a loving mom*—leads me to bust out laughing instead.

When a guy honks and cuts me off and shrieks at me, calling me a c-word, my hand does not automatically flip him the bird—a small change, maybe, but for me profound. That spring-loaded trigger has eased off. The guy's comment just flows past as if I've been lacquered over. Every so often I find myself praying for citizens like him though in the past I might have petitioned for a machine gun.

One morning at my desk, an essay I've had an idea about starts to unreel itself like a satin ribbon. Six hours later, I look up and realize I've been writing with ease.

Some days, premenstrual self-loathing can transform me into a ring-tailed, horn-honking, door-slamming bitch. But those incidents now strike me as 100 percent my problem, regardless of provocation. And they bring me to my knees, for it's on their back end that I sometimes fantasize about a slender glass of innocent champagne with some berry-colored crème de cassis making a little sunset in the flute's bottom.

Therapy rescued me in my twenties by taking me inward, leaching off pockets of poison in my head left over from the past. But the spiritual lens—even just the nightly gratitude list and going over each day's actions—is starting to rewrite the story of my life in the present, and I begin to feel like somebody snatched out of the fire, salvaged, saved.

II

Blooming after Loss

&

Shall the day of parting be the day of gathering?
And shall it be said that my eve was in truth my dawn?
—Kahil Gibran, The Prophet

Pushing Up the Sun

Kathy Rhodes

I close my hand around the cold, nickel knob and stop short. The Peggy's Cove picture has been hanging at eye level left of the front door for two years, since my trip to Nova Scotia that fell on the fifth anniversary of my husband's death. How many times did I walk past it taking the dog outside? I was always looking down toward the hardwood floor, putting on my shoes, leashing the spaniel, and I never really saw the scene until now.

Two gulls soar in a watercolor sky. Sea water swells, rages, rolls in, slams against giant boulders, and explodes high into ragged foam walls, splintered drops scattering, falling randomly back into self. One frothy column stretches higher than the lighthouse atop the rock, another smaller pillar of white beside it. Streaks of cerulean, orange, and yellow smear across the paper above a cobalt sea with whitecap curls. The lighthouse fades into a sunset, the smashing water the heart of the piece.

I've seen too many sunsets. Sunsets are ends—end of light, end of day, end of life.

The dog died last week—*our* dog, the puppy we picked out and raised together, loved and laughed over, the one who became my *reason* after Charlie was gone. She was almost seventeen at her end, and I held her withered body and whispered, "Go find your daddy." And then the light was gone, and the ocean raged in again, knocked me down, and carried me back to that first loss of the man I loved.

❧

Seven years ago on a Friday morning in June, I didn't know that, come Saturday, I wouldn't have a husband. I didn't know he had an aortic aneurysm that would eventually rupture from throat to groin. I didn't know he was bleeding out. He canceled customers, sat in his chair, the dog beside him, and tried to drink a cup of coffee with his usual nine squirts of Sweet & Low, but couldn't. That coffee sat on a table for the next nine months in all manner of green-gray, growing, velvet mold. I couldn't bear to throw it out.

The night he died, my sister arrived from Memphis, walked into my living room, and the first thing she said was, "You just have to build a whole new life." The words slammed against me cold. I hadn't yet realized I'd lost the old one.

But it was true. When his life ended, so did mine in many ways. While I held on to my identity as a writer, everything else was either gone or beginning to unravel—my job because I worked for him, our computer business, all sources of income, a house we built together, companionship, and future dreams.

Life had boiled what was in my crucible down to the salt of me.

The loss brought a feeling of being under water—everything murky and garbled. I struggled to rise up for breath, but my arms only floated in slow motion, unable to propel me. My hair streaked out all around me, curling in the rhythm of the water, and so did my dress. I couldn't gather everything back in close to me, smooth it down, and make it lie flat. I looked up at the surface to see sunny blues and greens, wavy, with white light shining and spearing down, creating milky colors, and I felt I would never be in that bright, happy place again.

I didn't want to start over. I was not in the building phase of life. In my fifties, I should be basking in the easy warmth of love, on the cusp of twilight years with my mate.

But I was a knocked-down mess. And I didn't have time to be a mess, with bills due, a funeral to plan, and a business to manage. I was a stinging mass of flesh and pulsing adrenaline with puppet legs that only moved when forced to.

At that time there were women who lost loved ones and wrote books about grief, and some even got movie deals and became famous. They hiked wilderness trails alone, drove around the country pulling a camper and baking pies, and traveled the world eating and praying and loving. Me? I did practical stuff because I had to pay bills and buy dog food. I couldn't go running around looking for something somewhere else.

In another new book, the author took to her bed and curled up in a fetal position for months. I couldn't do that either. I was the provider and had to take care of myself and the dog. I had to fast-forward—prepare a résumé, muddle through interviews, get a job, any job, earn a paycheck.

I cashed in a small life insurance policy to get by while I searched for work, and I closed Charlie's business, merging with another and contracting for three years of income for myself. Then I secured at an advertising agency what was probably the last job available to me before the crippling economic downturn hit full force.

Every morning, I got up and went to work, then came home to four walls closing in on me, cried, slept, and got up and did it again the next day. Six months went by, and I realized: He doesn't know I have this job, he doesn't know I work in Maryland Farms, he doesn't know my new boss or colleagues, he has never seen me in this black pin-striped blazer, he hasn't heard any of my work rants. I was building a whole new life, just like my sister had said.

After a year and a half, I lost that job when the company went under. In life it's never just one loss. Loss comes in layers that keep peeling down and eroding the person away.

So here I was again, starting over, with nothing. Somehow, even in my brokenness, I knew there was a reason for this. I knew it was my time to do something good for myself. Standing at the end of a line of fallen dominoes, I knew I needed to pull myself together, pick up my baggage, and press on.

∽

God uses broken things. Seeds break to produce new plants that make fruit or flowers. The seed comes from a plant that thrived in a season now gone. It lays dormant, tender parts packed inside a hard shell, all folded up. It needs water to soften it, needs warmth and sunshine, needs time. For the seed to achieve its ultimate purpose and become what it was destined to be, it has to come undone. The shell breaks, and the insides come out, and unfoldment occurs.

I was like the seed, folded up and packed tightly inside a hard shell, punched down into the darkness, dead at the end of my season with Charlie. I felt claustrophobic, confused, and anxious, with a heart thrumming, increasing in intensity, signaling a coming change away from this place I did not choose and did not understand.

By nature and need, I pushed the walls until they cracked and broke and fell into destruction, and parts of me began to come out into the new. Unfoldment was what I experienced. Growth didn't happen in a fast burst of activity. It was a process, and it was ongoing as I walked further into the light to see the person I was becoming.

My unfoldment came in cycles. My world had fallen into darkness, but the sun came up the next morning, because that's the way the universe works, and I had to get up, too, and take care of business. Summer went to autumn, then winter, cold and barren, when the world turned inward. And then spring came.

There was new life all around me that seemed to come out of nowhere, but I knew it had been latent and turbulent under the surface, waiting for the right time to come forth. I figure that's how life happens anew after loss—by following the cycles.

Nature expresses herself in circular patterns, from a simple bird's nest to the cycle of seasons to the cycle of life—birth, death, rebirth. I learned from that.

As time went by, padding formed between my loss and my present state. The early things I did routinely in order to float along kept me moving in circles—mundane things like getting the paper in every day, mowing the grass every week, paying the house note every first of the month, living from full moon to full moon. The revolutions spun me, and I realized that in carrying out all these tasks, I was moving on in a sea of people and daily transactions, not only moving around in circles but also moving forward in circles, taking the shape of a helix.

Like the seed parts, I was standing up, reaching out, and growing stronger. And like the plant, I was establishing a leaf system to absorb power and nutrients from the sun and strong roots to draw water from the source and hold me firmly through the winds.

∽

When I married for the second time at the age of forty-five, Charlie, who was forty-twelve, he'd noted, and who'd had a long, successful career with a Fortune 100 company before establishing his own business, told me, "I've lived my life. This marriage is about you."

For the first time ever, I had the freedom and support to get out there and be myself, to use my talents, and to write, submit, and get published in magazines, newspapers, and anthologies. I wrote a book and edited an anthology. I joined writers' groups and organizations and went to writing conferences. I served as president of my county's literary organization and on the board of directors of the state writers alliance. I created an online magazine for emerging and established writers, serving as publisher and editor, and, over an eight-year period, published the works of three hundred sixty-one writers from thirty-eight states and ten countries. It was all on a volunteer basis. I worked hard and did it for free. But I gained experience and even began to blossom a bit.

Life was easy when I depended on someone else who set a stage under me so I could perform. But with my husband gone, I had to figure out how the show would go on.

Could I turn my volunteer work into a real job? I needed it to generate an income. I knew that if I wanted a future with continuity, purpose, and happiness, I had to depend on myself, and not on others.

I was at equipoise, standing at the balance of past and future. It was a scary place, yet a generative one, with possibilities, sparks, colors, lightning, and creation, and I jumped onto the wave and rode it in.

This time, the planets aligned, and the stars were stepping stones. I made calculated choices and contacts, doors opened, and I built my tower block by block, stacking and arranging. All the decisions and experiences of my past came together. Undergraduate and graduate study in English grammar and literature, classroom teaching, marriage to an entrepreneur and the business acumen I had witnessed, volunteer work in the local and state writing community, knowing the right people, longtime dreams—everything fed into the flow. I took one step at a time, putting a foot forward on a cloud of hope and possibility, and it held me up. I began to spin life straight from my heart.

A permanent part-time job doing research, writing, and proofreading came quickly. Then came the opportunity to partner with an author I'd met at my previous job and start a business editing books, coaching writers, and teaching writing workshops.

I didn't know it then, but now I can look back and see my unfolding and flowering. Now, I am liking, no, loving myself. I am where I always wanted to be. Furthermore, at my happiest, I know that my Creator can yet soften, reshape, and redirect me. I know I can love again. I am still a woman with a supple heart.

On beginning again, I don't think that's something any of us sets out to do. I don't ever remember thinking, "Today, I'm going to begin again." I don't ever remember telling myself, "I've got to build a whole new life." I do think that after a period of time, when I stopped to look around and behind me, the beginning had happened. All I did was take care of the business at hand and move through my days doing what I had to do to keep my head above the smashing water. First I did what I had to do. Then I created what I wanted to do.

Someday, if not already, you, too, will lose someone close, someone who built your stage and held up your foundational walls, someone you lived with every day, someone you think you cannot live without. You will not completely get over the loss. You will learn to live with it, to encase the love, inlay it in your heart, and look on it smilingly. You will learn to rebuild. Most important, you will learn to be content in your current state and with yourself.

∾

I've had lots of sunsets, which means I've had lots of sunrises. It's a given that once the colors of sunset slip into obscurity, the sphere of light will come up again in a broadcast of color on the other side.

I love getting up early to watch the sun rise. I once watched it come up over the Atlantic on a flight from New York to Madrid, when Ruby Hilburn across the aisle threw a pillow at my head and told me to wake up and look out the window. I saw the first sunrise in the continental United States at Cadillac Mountain in Maine, when my sister and I got up at four and drove to the lookout point. I've watched a sunrise from the rim of the Grand Canyon. I've seen the sun come up over peaks of the Blue Ridge, Bitterroots, Smokies, Cascades, and Sangre de Cristos. I've watched it pour new rays over the Pacific as I stood on the wet sands of Oregon. And almost every morning, I watch it rise over the hills of Middle Tennessee. As the sky becomes aglow and separates from misty hills hidden in gray shadows, I see a familiar sight unfold. It looks just like sunset that happened only hours earlier. In a rose and cream mosaic sky, a pale yellow halo meets sapphire, and crowning rays of pearl reach out like the arms of God, illuminate, and give definition and truth I couldn't see before.

Sunrise is destined to happen. The earth moves us around through the dark until we can see the light again. We can sit and wait for what the light will bring to us, or we can stand up, be loud, and bring our talents and skills into the light and push and pull them along with us.

In the darkness after sunset, people often pray to God for sunrise—for healing, for the pain to end, for peace, for an open door, for something new and good. They want the destination, not the journey. No. Life gives us the journey. We've got to do the work. We've got to pull up the energy and put the feet to it. We've got to get in there, move around in the dark, deal with the pain, wait out the mourning, and, when it is time for sunrise, we've got to go and stand under it. Stand at the horizon of equipoise and put our hands under that ball of light and help push it up.

I think about the picture beside my front door of the lighthouse at Peggy's Cove. It sits against a pastel sky, high on a rock, visible from way out at sea, visible from across the room. In itself, it *is* a rock, a stronghold, a tower to those navigating tumultuous waters, a shining light that shows the way to go.

Now, with the fresh loss of *our* dog, I'm not going to sit around in the darkness after sunset, not going to linger in what was. I am going to follow the beam of light home over the smashing water. I'm getting a puppy, *my* puppy, a brand new dog to share my life.

I am standing under the sun and pushing it up.

Chapter 21

Jessica Handler
from Invisible Sisters

She took some twigs she found in the water and made a raft with a sail that she let dry. The sail was a peice [sic] of cloth. She sailed on 'til she came to land. —From a storybook Susie wrote and illustrated for Sarah, called "Mrs. Spider and the Giant," circa 1969

Mickey draws me while I sleep. He does this when we travel: on vacation, or visiting family, another time when an ice storm knocked our power out and we escaped the freezing darkness at home for a heated motel. He drew a picture of me on the wall of his study. I am awake in this one, depicted as a nearly life-sized cartoon superhero. I have heart-shaped insignia on my boots and on the clasp that holds my cape closed.

My husband did not know that when I was little, before Sarah was born and before Susie got sick, I sometimes pretended I was a hero who saved people in trouble. This seemed a rewarding way to live, magnanimous and kind, that would earn accolades I would modestly deny. Heroes save because they love. Trouble could be banished, never to return. I lived in a gentle world. As the first child and elder sister, my natural role was favored child and protector of the small. Hercules and Abiyoyo were my first role models. My grandfather and father replaced them, once I learned the stories of their real-life battles for justice. In time, my mother became my hero, although hers was a skill I could not easily emulate. Even in the worst circumstances, she made an effort to love life.

Observing the adults around me when Susie died, I noticed for the first time but not the last that survivors make one of two choices. Either the survivor caves in for the long term, or she decides to keep moving, as if living after the death of a loved one placed her on the kind of moving sidewalk you see in airports and shopping malls. Standing upright and holding the handrails would deliver her, at some future point, back into her life in progress. This is a decision that might not be made consciously. My family's survivors were one day startled to find that we had decided to keep moving.

There was no single moment when I made the choice not to cave in; I just stayed upright and held on. I held on in Los Angeles, warming my skin under the beachy glare. I held on at my mother's house the day of Sarah's funeral, when I confronted my father for leaving me. I held on when I bought the headstone for Susie's grave, and I held on during a summer night in Atlanta, peeling grease-spattered wallpaper printed with smiling teapots from my kitchen walls.

I first noticed that I had arrived at my life in progress when I caught myself talking in that empty kitchen. I lived alone: I was addressing myself. The act of talking to myself wasn't what startled me. What startled me was that I was happy.

There are times when I slip up, when time runs backward and I say without thinking, "I wish I were dead." I say this under my breath when a stack of paper slides off my desk, or I discover that the blouse I want to wear has lost a button, or I can't find a parking space and am running late. The words come in a monotone, triggered by a minor transgression.

When I catch myself saying these words, my heart races (clearly alive), and instinct claps my hands over my mouth. The "it" that eclipsed my family and terrified me when I was ten and eleven years old could still loiter over my shoulder, close enough to hear me.

Be careful what you wish for, my mother warns, without knowing my habit. She laughs when she says this. She is a habitual wisher, on pennies found face up or facedown, and on loose eyelashes caught with a fingertip. My mother dries the wishbones from chickens, and together we pull the brittle Y shapes apart. Silently, I wish to be fully alive, while my mother wishes for my desires to come true.

In my worst moods, I wonder why I am alive. Illness hid in my sisters' cells, but no disease has emerged from mine. You are alive just to *be* alive, I imagine Sarah saying. Susie, forever eight years old, concurs. You are alive because you are alive.

After Sarah died, I quietly appointed myself the curator of a family archive. At a moment's notice, I could put my hands on boxes of correspondence and photographs that my mother had kept, and a lifetime of my own keepsakes that I hauled from place to place for reasons I could not fully explain. I hoarded journals, yearbooks, and elementary school report cards. I put plastic food wrap around disintegrating copies of Atlanta's hippie newspaper, where ads for coffeehouses like the Twelfth Gate and a store that sold stash bags and peace flags preserved my father's era. I kept an answering machine tape with a message from Sarah. I kept a lumpy, cone-shaped clay figurine the color of dandelions that Susie made in kindergarten. I collected evidence, rescuing our past from oblivion. Each item was proof that our lost civilization had been real.

When I moved into my house, I shoved a heavy wooden cabinet into the too small guest room. The cabinet was poorly made and difficult to use; drawers fell off their tracks and could not be put back straight. The shelves were too narrow for storage. My parents had been given the cabinet as a wedding gift from a friend. When Sarah was a baby, it stood near her changing table. Mom stacked clean white cloth diapers in the drawers and piled safety pins with pink plastic tops on the shelves.

When I adopted the cabinet, the wood still smelled of baby lotion and furniture polish. I stored extra linens in the drawers, and cursed the broken runners whenever I needed a clean towel. After Mickey and I married, we decided to turn the guest room into a home studio. In order to streamline, we got rid of the cabinet. Mickey made sure it was hauled away when I was not home. I wept when I agreed to let the cabinet go. Hardly another death, I thought, but even so.

The memories hardest to live with are not furniture or art projects, but the ones I can't hold in my hands. My sisters loved me, and I loved them. I think of the ferocious, hot grip of Sarah's hug, and the brush of her tan winter coat cold against my skin as she propels me out of Harrisburg's small airport. She is sixteen, and her first driver's license is in her purse.

"Mom sent me to pick you up," Sarah says, bouncing on the balls of her feet. "She let me take her car."

We are crazy with excitement. I live in California, and she is still at home. We miss each other but have grown used to the fundamental difference that keeps us apart. We don't know how to tell each other how elated we are to be together.

Or I remember the weightless feeling that Susie and I got jumping on our parents' bed when we were six and four. I can feel the springs wobble inside the mattress. Susie and I bounce in our stocking feet, building momentum until we are airborne. We reach for the ceiling. Even flying we are too short to touch our fingertips to the flat white over our heads, and gravity pulls us down. We bend our knees to break the fall, but never enough, and we tumble backward, laughing as we roll into rumpled sheets.

A few years ago, I woke in the middle of the night to see Sarah silhouetted at the foot of my bed. I wasn't afraid.

I sat up and asked, "What is it?"

I reasoned that if I spoke as if nothing were unusual, nothing would be.

"What *is* it?" I repeated.

The shape shrugged in the same extravagant way that was Sarah's, and then turned and walked out the door. I didn't get out of bed to follow.

I see Susie less.

In high school, my girlfriends and I went through an Ouija board craze. After a few tries at contacting former pets and rock stars dead of overdoses, I went for Susie. This was against my better judgment, but the spirit of the moment won out. Sitting cross-legged on Mary Beth's bedroom floor, I asked the board about my sister. Where was she? Was she okay?

The planchette under my fingers spelled out "loves you."

My friends and I adjourned from the bedroom, shaken. We had stumbled from mere board game into questionable territory.

These might be brief brushes against what some people call "the other side," the place Sarah said she was heading when she coded, the place Susie sensed when she dreamed of an empty rocking chair. These are, more likely, how my longing for my sisters appears and reappears in my life, the same way the tide offers smooth-edge chunks of colored glass and unbroken, whorled shells.

Whole days can pass now when my sisters are not prominent in my thoughts. Most days, though, one or both of my sisters traverses my thoughts for the smallest of reasons. Two little girls, one dark haired and the other blonde, run hand in hand in front of me on the sidewalk, and I have to turn my head. A song comes on the radio that Sarah loved, and I want to call her and shout the chorus into the phone. In a different life, we would sing together before we complained that our favorite songs now play on oldies stations.

Every December, Mickey and I display Christmas and Chanukah cards on the fireplace mantel in our living room. We spend an evening writing ours, and happy as I am to send greetings to people I love, the fact that my sisters and I will exchange no cards hits me like a punch.

Mickey knows that I will get up from the boxes of cards and roll of stamps at the table and walk through our house alone a few times, as if I could escape tears. When I do come back to our table, my eyes are dry, and my pen is still in my hand. I am ready to pick up where I left off.

～

It's midnight in August 1974. I am up late, as usual. I am almost fifteen. My parents are asleep if they are both home, the TV blurting the eleven o'clock news, then Carson, then clicked off. If my father is not home, my mother has been reading in the bedroom she has made neat and tidy, with the radio turned to the classical station. She wipes Nivea cream on her face, one hand to each cheek, then places her book on her nightstand and turns out the light, free to dream. Sarah sleeps in her bedroom across the hall from mine. I am still dressed. I've been reading, lying on my stomach down the length of my bed, listening as the house goes quiet for the night. Now that my family is down, I am up. I have a spiral notebook in my lap and a pen in my hand. A coffee mug that I keep for an ashtray leans against my thigh. In preparation for writing, I have dumped the old cigarette butts into my trashcan and lit a fresh cigarette. My radio alarm clock is tuned where it always is, radio station WQXI, "Quicksie in Dixie." Eric Clapton sings, "I Shot the Sheriff."

I reach over and tug the chain on the desk lamp. The sudden yellow beam of light makes me shield my eyes for a second. I have a lot to write tonight.

I do not write about marriage, or the perfect job, or kids. I do not write about what I want to come true when I grow up. I don't know this yet, but I am writing messages and sending them away in bottles that will wash up on a future shore where I will find them when I am an adult.

"I am so glad for the journals," I wrote. "It's like a memory bank."

My journals affirm that I was there, too. I was there, diligently recording my existence on the page, reminding myself that I mattered. Death is permanent, but I knew without daring to admit it that living while drowning in dread can be temporary.

I knew then that my family's rough voyage would end. When it did, my compass needle would wobble, then settle, and point in the direction where I would find myself. I had devoted myself to trying to save people I loved, obscuring what I knew: that I loved myself, too. I could not save my sisters, but in my journals, I worked to save myself.

Years before Sarah spoke the words, I knew without being told that I would be the only one left. Who else would I be then, when I became sisterless? I would be the memory keeper, admiring the glinting beauty of my sisters' lives and the promise in what our family had been. As I admired, I taught myself to see me again: the visible sister, with days behind me and days wide open ahead.

My Brother's Keeper

Julie Cantrell

Then the LORD said to Cain, "Where is your brother Abel?"
"I don't know," he replied. "Am I my brother's keeper?"
—Genesis 4:9

I was four years old when I got the call that I had a baby brother. I can still remember the next-door neighbor handing me the kitchen phone. I coiled its harvest-gold cord around my wrist, looking up to her as she said, "It's a boy!" My entire body reacted. There was no better gift than a baby brother of my very own. And oh, the possibilities were endless! I would teach him to talk and walk and tie his shoes. I would put him in costumes and give him parts in my plays and I would make him fetch! He would be the best pet ever. Way better than a puppy. And he was mine. All mine.

But the desire to boss him quickly morphed into a desire to love and protect him. Even at four, I knew Jeff was special. Anchored by those magical eyes, he was crowned with sugar-white curls atop a muscular body of golden skin. By the time he was a toddler, he already had sculpted abs and rock-hard biceps. He looked like a little man, thundering through life with the energy of a lightning bolt. He was both heaven-sent and hard to handle, and through the years he was assigned labels that ran the extremes. He was admired for his artistic and athletic talents, but his temper would sometimes reveal his darker nature. He was fabulously flawed, funny yet furious. But most of all, he was loved. By his mother and father, by his friends and coaches, and particularly by me, his sister.

There is something powerful about the sibling bond. Perhaps that's why it is a recurring theme throughout the human narrative. Sibling relationships are both mythical and biblical, but even the earliest storytellers understood the power of a page-turner. That's why we only need to read to the fourth chapter of Genesis to see sibling rivalry at its worst. This is where Cain kills his brother Abel, committing the first murder, and then he lies to the great Creator about his jealous act, sarcastically taking a jab at God with his snide remark about being his brother's keeper.

Whether we were told Bible stories or Greco-Roman myths, many of us have grown up learning about the bitter battles between Jacob and Esau, Joseph and his brothers, or Romulus and Remus. These are the tales we remember because sibling rivalry creates more tension in the plot than any tale of healthy relationships.

But there are other stories, much less told. The myth of the twins, Castor and Pollux, for example, who were so close as brothers that when Castor was killed, Pollux offered to share his own godly immortality with his minor brother. This selfless gesture inspired Zeus to place the brothers together in the heavens where they continue to shine today as the two brightest stars in the Gemini constellation.

Together, Castor and Pollux are believed to send a guiding light known as St. Elmo's Fire, signaling sailors to safety on the stormy seas. Scientifically speaking, St. Elmo's Fire is an electrical discharge typically observed around high points such as masts, poles, and spires. The glow has been compared to fireworks, stars, coronas, and sparks, and it sometimes generates a distinct sound, much like crackling.

Christopher Columbus and Charles Darwin documented St. Elmo's Fire in their journals, and the phenomenon has been recorded since the earliest works of literature. Julius Caesar, Pliny the Elder, and Herman Melville are just a few of the authors who were inspired by this light-based spirit of the sea. Even William Shakespeare wrote the following lines in *The Tempest* (I.ii.196–201):

ARIEL:
I boarded the king's ship; now on the beak,
Now in the waist, the deck, in every cabin,
I flamed amazement: sometime I'd divide,
And burn in many places; on the topmast,
The yards and bowsprit, would I flame distinctly,
Then meet and join.

Pliny the Elder, in his second book of *Natural History*, described St. Elmo's Fire as stars that appeared both on land and sea:

I have seen a light in that form on the spears of soldiers keeping watch by night upon the ramparts. They are seen also on the sail-yards, and other parts of ships, making an audible sound, and frequently changing their places. *Two* of these lights forebode good weather and a prosperous voyage, and extinguish *one* that appears single and with a threatening aspect—this the sailors call *Helen*, but the two they call *Castor and Pollux*, and invoke them as gods. These lights do sometimes, about evening, rest on men's heads and are a great and good omen.

As Shakespeare and Pliny described, the mythical glow can divide into two (the twin brothers) and can move from place to place. But one of the most fascinating characteristics is that St. Elmo's Fire usually occurs near the end of a thunderstorm, suggesting clearer weather is soon to come. Thus, a visit by this saintly spirit is seen as a blessing, a reason to hold on to hope when life becomes scary and uncertain.

Like the twin brothers who serve as the guardians of St. Elmo's fire, the flame represents the good of the world. And this is what a sibling relationship is supposed to offer us too, a source of constant companionship and balanced support, as we see between Castor and Pollux. A reminder that one person will always be by our side in this life, especially when the storms swell against us.

In *The Sibling Bond*, Stephen Bank and Michael Kahn wrote that the sibling relationship "lasts longer than our relationship with our children, certainly longer than with a spouse, and with the exception of a few lucky men and women, longer than with a best friend."

And it isn't just the fact that more than fifty percent of our genes are the same. It's the experience of sharing a childhood that seals the deal. These life experiences create a basic understanding of one another that no one else will ever have. No matter how much we may argue or differ or even hurt each other, no one will ever understand us or know us better than a sibling who shared our youth. There is an unspoken link of sameness. It is the unbreakable sibling bond.

Jeffrey Kluger, author of *The Sibling Effect: What the Bonds among Brothers and Sisters Reveal about Us*, has said that our siblings are our "collaborators and co-conspirators, our role models and cautionary tales. They are our scolds, protectors, goads, tormentors, playmates, counselors, sources of envy, objects of pride. They teach us how to resolve conflicts and how not to; how to conduct friendships and when to walk away from them. Sisters teach brothers about the mysteries of girls; brothers teach sisters about the puzzle of boys."

This is what we learn from sharing life with a sibling. We learn how to live and how to love.

So if I am my brother's keeper, what does it say about me that my brother didn't live to see twenty?

～

"Brothers and sisters are as close as hands and feet."

—Vietnamese Proverb

Before we get to the end, let's go back to the beginning. On March 1, 1978, a baby boy broke his way into the world, blue and silent. Not a sound to be heard. The medical team scrambled around him, eager to kick-start his lungs into action, anxious to help oxygen find its way to his brain.

Thanks to fast action and plenty of prayers, the much-anticipated and already-adored infant began to breathe. His skin yellowed, his voice was found, and he opened his bright blue eyes, two beauties that would soon become a haunting hazel, shifting with the background and someday working wonders on the ladies with their signature chameleon charm.

The baby was given a name: Jeffrey Michael. The latter was the name of his father. The first was selected so that his initials could be monogrammed in sync with my own: JMP. We were siblings, and like Castor and Pollux, we were on each other's side in this world. A pair.

The night I got the call about my brother's death, I was twenty-three years old. He had celebrated his nineteenth birthday the night before. My mother had baked his favorite cake and given him a few simple presents. I had been trying to reach him for three days straight, but he had been out with friends—at the movie theater, a party, the river, a bonfire. He had a lot of friends. I had left messages, singing "Happy Birthday" off-key with an exaggerated *I love you* at the end of each recording.

This was long before texting, and people weren't accessible twenty-four/seven as we are now. It was no big deal to wait for someone to return a call, but it was his birthday weekend and I had the flu, along with major sister-guilt for not being at my mother's house to snap photos and watch him open gifts. I was an hour away with my husband in our own home, trying to go to bed early and muster the strength to get through the following workday despite fighting fever and chills.

Before calling it a night, I tried one more time to reach my brother. A senior in high school, he had only a couple months left until graduation and still lived at home with our mother. My mom answered. I heard Jeff talking in the background, and I asked to speak with him. He wasn't in the mood. He had always been "edgy"—an unpredictable storm of extremes. He could be loving and gentle, funny and charming, but on a whim he could snap into a fury that would intimidate even the strongest of men. My mother and I had long walked on eggshells, as we had always done with my father who passed more than his glassy eyes to my brother's genes. This was one of those moments when we both knew to steer clear. Jeff needed to use the phone. Needed to call a girl. And so he did.

I didn't know that would be the last time I ever heard my brother's voice, a muffled echo from across the room, telling my mother he needed the phone. I'd never again have the chance to wish him happy birthday, to tell him about the gift I had bought him, to say I love you one more time.

I let my mother go, took a shower, pulled my hair into a ponytail, and brushed my teeth. I took care of a few chores and folded some laundry. I was eager to crawl beneath the covers and rest my aching body. But before I could find the pillow, the phone rang. It was a landline phone, located in the front office of our home. I stumbled toward the room, my feet dragging against the wooden floor, as cool drafts of air wafted between the ancient seams. It took four, maybe five rings for me to answer.

"Julie?"

I recognized the Filipino accent right away. My stepmother, Cora, was on the other end of the line. She had never called me before, and she never has since.

I greeted her by asking, "What's wrong?"

"Jeff. Shot. Head." English is not her native language, and in the shock of the trauma, she struggled to find words.

The string of sounds made no sense to me. Was my brother shot in the head? Did he shoot someone else in the head? What was happening?

"Is he alive?" These are the words that surfaced.

"No." Her answer left me cold.

I dropped the phone. It bounced across the wooden floor with a thud, like a scene in the movies. I tried to yell for my husband. My vocal cords could not form sound. My legs were weak. My hands were shaking.

My brother was dead.

I found the phone beneath the desk and tried to dial my mother's house. It took me five tries, maybe six. My fingers couldn't find the right buttons. My brain couldn't remember the familiar numbers. My muscles could not perform the simple task. It never occurred to me to hit Redial. Finally, I managed the call. The phone rang. My mother answered. Her voice was hollow. Numb. But it meant she was still alive, and this allowed me my first breath since Cora broke the news. The relief was palpable.

"Is he alive?" I asked the same question, hoping for a different answer this time.

"No." She could not bring herself to say more.

"I'm on my way."

By now my husband had joined me in the office, a pinched concern between his brows. "Jeff's dead!" I shouted, even though he was less than two feet from me. "Jeff's dead!" I yelled again, still trying to absorb this new truth. I threw on a pair of jeans and pulled a sweatshirt over the t-shirt I had been wearing for bed. Then I flew to the truck, barefooted, braless, and breathless.

My husband drove, flashing his hazard lights all the way from Fordoche, Louisiana, to East Baton Rouge. The trip to my mother's house should have taken an hour. We made it in less than thirty minutes.

Along the way, I needed more information. I found my cell phone and tried to call my mother again, but the battery was dead—something that never happened to me, as I was obsessive about keeping it charged in case of emergency. The frustration caused me to scream and throw the phone at the floorboard. I couldn't sit back against my seat. I leaned, anxious, toward the front windshield, wishing I could make the truck move faster, wishing I didn't live so far from home, wishing I had been there to stop this from happening.

I had grabbed my shoes on the way out the door, so I put them on in the truck, tying and retying the laces, frustration building with every failed attempt.

When we finally turned into my mother's subdivision, cars were already parked in the street by her house. Police cars, ambulances, and other vehicles lined the quiet lane. Yellow and black crime scene tape had been stretched across the front yard. My husband slowed the truck, trying to find a place to park. I couldn't wait another second. I jumped from the moving vehicle and raced up the concrete driveway. A female cop in white gloves stretched out her hand to stop me. "He's my brother!" I yelled, and then again, "He's my brother!"

She stepped aside, and I ran to the back door of my mother's home. As I turned the corner, I saw friends gathered beneath the carport, on the patio, huddled in tight circles, whispering. Crying. Some stared at me, grief in their eyes. Others looked away, uncomfortable.

I was angered. Shamed that they had managed to get here before me. This was my mother. My brother. My family. And they had arrived first.

I opened the squeaky screen door, and then the French-paned entry that led to the crowded living room. My mother had been a single mom, raising two children on a humble school-teacher's salary. Her home was a quaint three-bedroom brick ranch that had been filled with love and laughter and friends and food. She had done her best. We all knew that. Her life had not been easy, but she had made ours as nice as she possibly could. We never lacked for food, shelter, kindness, or support.

And now, in return, Jeff had dealt her the cruelest hurt imaginable. I was angry.

I shuffled my way through the swarm of friends, law enforcement, church members, and neighbors. Why were all these people here? This was a private matter! That's what I wanted to say. I wasn't even wearing a bra. The last thing I had expected was a crowd. But I stayed silent, searching for my mother.

When I saw her, she was pale and shaking, standing at the kitchen counter where Jeff's birthday cake sat half-eaten, candle holes still visible in its shell. Someone was handing her a pill and a glass of water. My mother allowed no drugs, no alcohol, no tobacco in our home. She had been brought up in the conservative Southern Baptist faith and had brought us up the same way, so to see her accept an anxiety pill from a friend's hand suggested I had lost her too. When she looked up at me, I knew this was true. She carried the half-dead stare of a person whose soul had been shattered. Slivers of her spirit had been sent spiraling away from bone, splintered into a storm of shards. In that moment, I knew I would spend the rest of her life chasing them down for her, gathering all the pieces I could find. But she would never feel whole again. This I knew.

I pulled my mother into a hug but she was cold, limp. She had no love to offer me in that moment. And no matter how much I poured into her, it could never fill the hole.

The preacher called us all together, asking us to hold hands, to pray. I was angry. I was angry at Jeff, at the preacher, at God. I was angry at my father and all the people who had gathered in our home to offer support. Mostly I was angry at myself, for not protecting my little brother. For not keeping him safe and alive in this world. I was angry.

As everyone bowed their heads and closed their eyes, I scanned the room. My mother's friends, my brother's friends, our family friends, our church friends. All here, all because they loved Jeff. And he could never see it. He didn't believe his life was worth living. He couldn't see through the pain.

The paramedics carried his body in a black bag from his bedroom, my bedroom actually, because he had given up his own for a friend who needed a temporary place to stay. The men moved through the narrow hallway, turning awkwardly to make the angle into the small foyer and out the front door. What an unusual way for him to leave, I thought. Horizontal, rather than vertical. Out the front, rather than the back. As a teen, rather than an old man.

Everything was skewed. Nothing made sense.

"If you have a brother or sister, tell them you love them every day—that's the most beautiful thing. I told my sister how much I loved her every day. That's the only reason I'm okay right now." — *Amaury Nolasco*

The day after he turned nineteen, my brother put his hunting shotgun to his head and pulled the trigger. He made the choice that his life was no longer worth the hurt. In a split second, he ended his own pain by transferring it to those who loved him most. It took me a while to forgive him.

Nothing about suicide is fair. Or easy. Or rational. Nothing about it is clean or peaceful or understandable. And it leaves loved ones behind to carry the ache, a loss too immeasurable for words. Even for a writer.

But in time I did forgive my brother. I forgave him and not only came to understand his choice but also to empathize with his decision. He saw no other way through the dark depths of depression. He had seen counselors, taken medications, and altered his diet. He had turned to football, gym workouts, boxing matches. He had turned to music and to art and to hard blue-collar labor jobs that left him exhausted from working after class dismissed. He had many friends who kept him busy and social and engaged. He relied on humor and was always the one making everyone laugh. He had tried everything. Even faith. But life had been hard on him, and he had become convinced that he was never going to get a break. He was the unlucky, ill-fated loser of the world who would always find a way to make a mess of things. That's what he believed. It wasn't the case, but no matter how much we tried to get him to see himself as we saw him, he couldn't see his own truth.

Somewhere along the way, my brother had begun to believe lies about himself. Lies that told him he was worthless, a screw-up, a person who hurt the ones who loved him. He began to believe we'd all be better off without him. It didn't matter that he had a loyal tribe of friends who loved him fiercely, spraying graffiti on the high school gymnasium the night of his death, determined not to let him go gently into that dark night. It didn't matter that he had a family who had rallied around him, taking him to specialists and therapists and pharmacists and vacations and practices and tutoring sessions and church. It didn't matter that he had tremendous talents and that opportunities were about to unfold for him.

One week after my brother's death, my mother received word that Jeff had been hired at the Department of Wildlife and Fisheries. It was his dream job. And he had landed it. If only that news had come sooner. If only he had held on a few days. Life would have shifted and he would have had reason to hope again. But he didn't hold steady in the storm. He didn't wait to see St. Elmo's Fire. And worst of all, I wasn't there to save him.

My brother died nineteen years ago. He would be thirty-eight years old now, an image I struggle to generate. I will always see him as a nineteen-year-old high school football star and boxing champion, carting coolers of fish from the river into my mother's kitchen, working on his fixer-upper pickup truck in the driveway of her humble home. I will always hear his gruff voice, telling crude jokes and laughing only after the rest of the room responds to his humor. I will always hear the Willie Nelson CD he was playing when he died, and the lyrics will forever bring me some sense of peace, knowing he was not alone in the moment he pulled that trigger: "I thought about you, Lord. I thought about you."

In the end, my brother did not "commit" a crime. He did not even die of "suicide." His life was cut short by the overwhelming force of depression. These word choices matter because when someone finds out that my brother "committed suicide," it's all they hear. It's all they know of him. And there is so much more to him than that one split-second decision.

Jeff lived nineteen years of full intensity. He laughed and he loved. And he was loved greatly by many. He lived a full life, more so than many people I know who have lived much longer. He packed a lot into those two short decades, and his spirit will forever be a part of my own.

Today, as I consider the timeline of my life, I see a series of fault lines, before and after marks that signal the touch points or torch points of my journey. My brother's birth and death are two such marks, contradicting one another with a spike and a sink. But in between the high and low, there were nineteen years of waves. Each one rising and crashing. Each one bringing me out into this great big world, transporting me to new places and new people. Offering me new opportunities to grow and learn.

Despite the fact that Jeff's life ended much too soon, I don't think of my brother as being dead. Instead, I believe he is experiencing a second bloom of sorts, somewhere out there in this vast universe of ours. Truly, in the eternal and infinite scheme of time and space, there is not much separating Jeff and me. So instead of grieving his passing or focusing on the missing pieces in my life, I choose to picture my brother shining his star beside my own, the two brightest lights in our own private constellation.

Sometimes, the storms of life hit full force, and the seas become rough. In those times, Jeff and I divide and move separately for a while, like Castor and Pollux becoming two. But just when I start to feel unsafe and abandoned, I listen for the crackle on the mast and I watch for the parallel glow of St. Elmo's Fire. If I look hard enough, he is always there to be found, my patron saint, my brother, my closest companion, lighting the way in the storm. Reminding me to hold on to hope. That I am never alone.

"There's no other love like the love for a brother. There's no other love like the love from a brother." —Terri Guillemets

The Widow Wessman

NancyKay Sullivan Wessman

Now seventy-two, with long, more-white-than-blonde hair in a stylish Swedish braid, Margy still smiles at the recollection of her engaging ten-year-old self and recalls, "My brother did magic tricks." Girlfriends had gathered that cold February day for her very special birthday party on Chadbourne Road in Shaker Heights, Ohio. Mother Wessman served punch and cake, probably pink, as that's her favorite color, and then the girls daintily seated themselves on the big Persian rug to see the magic show.

Fifteen and fascinatingly handsome to the little girls, R. Livingston Wessman grinned as he introduced his audience to the magic of illusion. Carefully setting his stage, he whipped out silk scarves, making them disappear and then reappear. He performed card tricks, and they could not figure out how he did them so fast. With long, straight fingers and a quick flex of his wrist, he made money bend and then return to normal.

Forty years later and nearly a thousand miles to the south, still smiling with the bluest of eyes and sporting a wax-tipped, handlebar mustache, Dick Wessman made magic for me, too. Magic not in a deceptive or illusionary way but magic as in new, charming and enlightening, supernatural, and definitely superior. Near the second anniversary of my having bought a two-bedroom, two-bath house with a brick courtyard and loft overlooking a triple French-doored gallery, I had almost finished lawn and gardening work for that hot Saturday. No makeup, pink-and-orange hat barely covering sweaty hair, ragged work clothes, I wondered why the mailman was pulling to a stop alongside my curb. To chat, to reconnect eighteen years after we first met through Sports Car Club of America (SCCA) rallies and parties, to suggest we get a beer and talk over old times.

"Oh, I'm divorced now," Dick announced before pulling away to finish his mail deliveries for the day.

"Well, I certainly hope so if you're asking me for a date," I replied.

Eleven months later, I joined him near the altar at St. James' Episcopal Church, and we became wife and husband—I his third, he my first. Although I had already migrated from Southern Baptist to Episcopalian, Dick, with his Methodist background, initiated our churchgoing only a few weeks into our dating; he was confirmed in our first full year together. Before the wedding, our priest asked why we wanted to marry each other. "Because I love him," I naively but honestly replied, and he said, "Because we have fun together." That perfect day in May, in the presence of God, family, and friends, I suddenly realized I had married three men and a dog.

Three men and a dog—Dick and his two sons, twenty-two and twenty years of age, and Mr. Tubbs, his twelve-year-old guard dog from hell, a knee-high yellow dog who also sported a big mustache, bushy brows, and eager eyes. George Stanley Tubbs Wessman lived with us until he reached nineteen and a half years, and his remains in a brass urn inscribed "Mr. Tubbs—Damn Good Dog" now float on a shelf in the den.

No individual ever really marries another single somebody. Everybody comes with associated people or stuff—experiences, belongings, expectations. But nobody had prepared me for all those men, those male creatures, nor for the steep learning curve—from me, my, mine to we, our, ours. Self-described to the new men in my life as "a very successful old maid career woman," I no longer lived alone, planned holidays just for myself, or impulsively decided to travel with Girlfriend Margaret to Nova Scotia or British Columbia. My family life expanded to include not only Dick's sons but also his sister Margy and her family, his cousins in Ohio, and his fraternity brothers from Tucson, Arizona, to Abingdon, Virginia. We also embraced the mother of our sons, her new husband, and her siblings and their families in Michigan, California, Oregon, and Africa. No longer limited to McAlpins and Sullivans, my life expanded to encompass not only the adults but also the children as they matured, married, and brought babies into our world.

People and personal relationships beyond family came via longtime friends, some shared and some newly acquired, through church, from work, and in a burgeoning renaissance community called Fondren. We outgrew my little house and moved a mere mile away to a mid-century ranch house with a big yard and many trees. We added a screened porch on the back, transformed a walk-through bedroom into an office, and updated the front entrance. Dick's remark on a visit to Selbey Gardens in Sarasota, Florida, that he wanted our place to resemble a tropical oasis opened opportunities for my mother and me to populate our space with collected and pass-along plants from throughout central Mississippi. The Arizona-Sonora Desert Museum and botanical garden in Tucson prompted a cactus collection of sorts, including a welcoming iron sculpture saguaro that greets guests near our front door.

Marking our travels on a big United States map made for interesting conversation and magical memories. A Rand McNally *Road Atlas* delivered for Dick's playing the SCCA St. Valentine's Day Massacre Road Rally in 1997 provided our official travel record: orange highlights road trips from South Florida and the east coast of Georgia and South Carolina across Texas and the Southwest to San Diego and Los Angeles, upward to Colorado, across to St. Louis, northward through Chicago, to Green Bay, and around the Upper Peninsula and then southward along the east coast of Lake Michigan, finally squiggling over

Indiana, Ohio, New York, Pennsylvania, West Virginia, Kentucky, and Tennessee, then back to Alabama, Mississippi, Arkansas, and Louisiana. Blue highlights Amtrak travel from Jackson to Chicago and then west to Seattle and Vancouver, to San Francisco, east to New York City and Boston, and, distinctly, from Jackson to New Orleans for trips northeast to Washington, DC, and to Boston, and again southwest to Los Angeles.

Although neither of us much cared for flying, that was the only way we could get to Sweden and Norway, to Paris, to Eastern Europe for a riverboat cruise from Budapest to Bucharest, to Ireland for a transatlantic voyage aboard the *Queen Mary 2* back to the United States, and to Buenos Aires, Argentina, for sailing around the southernmost point on the globe and northward to Santiago, Chile, for Christmas 2007.

Dick Wessman made the magic as we balanced careers and church, home and family, friends and trips, and as we advanced from full-time work into early retirement. For fifteen years, we marveled at our most-surely-fated marriage—how otherwise would such a super-smart and totally handsome playboy from Ohio via the University of Arizona land in Jackson, Mississippi, to wed a country girl journalist-become-public health PR director? Our worlds were too different, too far apart. He, the adventurer, the fun-loving, spontaneous charmer matched to an asserter, an earthy, energetic, loyal, and protective sort. Even at our worst—I controlling, self-centered, and sometimes insensitive to his often unfocused, rebellious, and self-destructive self—we were perfectly mated.

Mother Wessman had identified the dominant personality trait for Dick's dad, who immigrated to the United States from Munkfors, Sweden, as a young lad of nine. Carl Oké Wessman, who spoke not a word of English upon his family's arrival in Detroit, Michigan, would graduate at the top of his high school class in Cleveland, Ohio, and excel at Northwestern University,

Evanston, Illinois. Handsome, deliberate, self-confident, and "a damn stubborn Swede," according to Edith Wedow Wessman. Their son shared his father's truest characteristics, followed in his stamp-collecting steps, and amassed other "toys": collections also of coins, kachinas, pots and baskets, frog and owl fetishes, toy soldiers, books, kaleidoscopes—his every interest magical to me.

How could it have ended so quickly, and how could I not have prevented his too-soon death? Maybe I was in deep denial of the dangers inherent in life too well lived: abundance of good food and drink, over-adequate enjoyment of all play, generosity of the Universe for happiness, joy, and life. Richard Livingston (Dick) Wessman, seventy-two, died Friday, November 5, 2010, at St. Dominic Hospital after a brief acute illness and in the presence of family and close friends. His zest for life focused on sports, arts and crafts, reading, and travel. His passion for sports cars led him to become first pro rally director of the Sports Car Club of America (SCCA); a master's-level city and urban planner, he was also a longtime member of the Board of Directors of the Mississippi Region, SCCA. Always a supporter of craftsmen and artists, he patronized their organizations and volunteered his time to support their talents. A resident of Fondren and a communicant of St. James' Episcopal Church, he volunteered at the University of Mississippi Medical Center ICU and the Mississippi Crafts Center.

What should or could I have done differently? If only I had demanded more visits to the doctor before that final trip to the ER, with more attention to discovering and treating the condition that caused the low-grade fever and undiagnosed infection. I was not ready for him to go and for me to have to learn to live without him.

Thank God, we who were not young when we married had discussed the possibility of just such an insidious event, the possibility that either of us could suddenly and inexplicably be hooked up to life-sustaining tubes and other equipment in the sterile atmosphere of a hospital. Both of us told the other, "Pull the plug." Dick had demanded more: "Pull the plug or just shoot me." In the end, he had lived a good, hard, hearty life, and he avoided frailty and incapacity. He was not an invalid. Thanks be to God.

A church friend and valued psychotherapist reviewed our experiences. "What you and Dick had, NancyKay," she told me, "was a fifteen-year love affair. For you, every day was Christmas."

Christmas. The beginning. And Easter. Eternity.

But what about me—what could I do then, what would I do next? What can I do even now, some five-plus years later, while recalling that magical time, that time of total freedom I enjoyed to shower unconditional love upon my very own damn stubborn Swede? Daily life was not perfect; we stressed, we learned to disagree, to argue, to fight like dogs and let the fur fly, as Dear Friend Margaret describes. We learned to kiss and make up, too, to get over the difficult times and relish the love and life we had together. During those years with Wessman, I fully possessed what some believe to be the deepest desire of every human heart, the opportunity to unconditionally love and be loved.

Now I continue. Dubbed during an early and unconventional grieving episode as The Widow Wessman, I live in our home, surrounded by his, mine, ours, all the things we brought into this space: wall art, collected objects crafted by indigenous peoples and skilled artisans, books written by Southerners and other world-class authors. Sometimes I describe it all as Dick Wessman's museum, but return trips to the Southwest have shown me that I, too, choose all this stuff to be in my home, to reflect the experiences we shared and show visitors the belongings that give me joy. I wear the wonderful old pawn and contemporary jewelry he gifted to me. I marvel at how he helped me trust, learn to be more nearly gentle, and value the spirit. I appreciate that he taught me to chill, to relax, to settle down, to be.

I read, and I write. Although I could hardly compose a sentence, much less a paragraph, in those first three years after Dick's death, I resumed research, continued studying the business of books, and finished a how-to guide for parents to apply lessons learned in the Bogalusa Heart Study toward growing their own heart-healthy children. Founding researcher Dr. Gerald Berenson and I self-published in 2012, and two years later I finally returned to the emergency response stories I had begun researching in 2008. I determined to finish writing and publish *Katrina, Mississippi: Voices from Ground Zero* before the tenth anniversary of the horrific hurricane's assault on the Mississippi Gulf Coast. Attentive to first responders' tales and immersing myself in their emergency operations center, I pushed to create a novel reading experience. Commemorating Katrina and celebrating what I call "champions of the storm," friends from six states joined me to launch the book with a wine and cheese party at the Gulfport Galleria of Fine Art–Carnegie Library on July 25, 2015.

This writing life differs markedly from newspaper journalism, public relations, health education and communications. Early in the book-writing business, I realized my need to study, to embrace a broader perspective, to change my usual staccato style into a deeper delving, greater exploration, and use of varied techniques to tell bigger stories. Along the writing path, I competed to secure one of fifty spots in the 2011 *Oxford American*'s Summit for Ambitious Writers; studied the genre of creative nonfiction in workshops and conferences; and traveled annually to Texas for Kathy Murphy's Girlfriend Weekend, where heralded and emerging authors plus readers from some 600 affiliated book clubs gather each January to celebrate literacy. From the book launch for *Katrina* to successful signings throughout Mississippi and in nearby Fairhope, Alabama, I shared the spotlight as one of Murphy's 2016 Select Authors to speak and sign at Girlfriend Weekend, and I look forward to sharing stories for many years of those individuals who told me about their emergency preparedness and response work before, during, and after Hurricane Katrina. Readers have commented that the book is "written so well you can smell the odor of rotting fish, rancid pork bellies, raw sewage and more...feel in awe of the dedicated responders and the courage of the victims. This book is a page turner...." *Yes!* And I am grateful.

Not long after Dick died, another dear friend who lives in West Virginia and had months earlier lost her own later-in-life husband sent me a book, *Life After Loss: A Practical Guide To Renewing Your Life After Experiencing Major Loss* (Bob Deits, M.Th.). Three words in the first chapter rang true and gave me more hope for a future without him than any other I can recall: "Every marriage ends...."

Alone again. Before marriage, I lived alone, and I had little patience with elderly relatives who also lived alone after decades of marriage but complained about it. I did not realize how loud the quietness can be. I did not truly know the meaning of "alone." In this situation I attempted to find my future as a single woman, to restore balance, to be. In my quest, I embraced church service with a different focus, attended a dream workshop, and began to explore the Enneagram, an ancient personality typing system that attempts to explain why and how people behave. Approaching the Enneagram as an important tool to improve relationships, deepen spirituality, and enable transformation, I have learned that my essential personality is one of strength, assertiveness, and protection. Even though I despise hearing individuals trying to console me with, "But you're so strong!" I know that I can be resourceful, decisive, and self-reliant. I can employ this tool to examine dark, challenging aspects of my personality and to grow spiritually and experience transformation.

I do desire spiritual growth and transformation. I aspire to being a better person, achieving my intellectual and sacred potential, attaining better health, living a long, disease-free life. That's why I've devoted more time and space to reading the words of other writers in both religious and secular realms. I have sought to learn from them as I become more intentional, more mindful, more productive. I aim to de-clutter and deeply clean my living space. I want to focus more on gardening and less on yard work. I want to be tall and thin, but I also want to cook, entertain, and eat, drink, and be merry. I want to schedule time for physical exercise, exploration of art, and meditation; I want to do all those things. I want to write, and I want to return to piano playing. I want to figure out how to become whoever-the-hell or under-heaven woman I am supposed to be. I want to grow beyond navel-gazing to create, to attain artist status, to contribute, to influence, to connect, to develop relationships. I want to surprise myself.

In this more-familiar-than-not new phase as a once-again-single woman, I, The Widow Wessman, choose to continue. I would never have chosen to be widowed. Having fully experienced the magic of Wessman, however, I know that I can, and I choose to channel his spirit with my strengthened will to live, create, and publish my own magic.

Root

River Jordan

Author's Note: When asked if I'd be interested in contributing to an anthology about women and their resurrection after loss or life changes, I said yes without hesitation. I've lived seven lives of a cat. I know a resurrected life, a season's change. I've been in one of the most difficult dark, death experiences of my life: what I would consider the death of my final marriage after roughly twenty years. But as I went to the page, considered my circumstances and what was old in me, what I discovered was that there is a strength that runs through my veins that is beyond me. It is the story and strength of my grandmother, of my mother, and it is these women, their stories, that bring me to my present day. I am the stuff of them. They had difficult, hard lives. They suffered loss upon loss in layers, but still they came up spades. Sometimes by their own strong hand, sometimes by a miracle. Always with a grace that astounds me. It is their begin again that inspires me, reminds me, that my life has indeed died in many ways or "gone to husk," but that eternal life of seed and resurrection will call me from this self-built tomb. Here in this short lyrical essay I've tried to paint in evocative language their dying and their rising so that I might cling to that seed of all that is good, all that is them, inside of me and believe yet that the light will drive out this shattering dark spot on my life. Had I written anything else, it would have been in volumes not easily given over to anthology.

Estelle

She didn't kill him. It's the first thing you should know, but fifty years was forty-nine too many. He was sorry, shiftless but satisfied with his own image. He carried secrets in one pocket, dice always jangled in the other. But this isn't his story.

Estelle made up ten of him. She bore eight children with his name, lost one at birth and birthed another. Worked all her life in peanut mills and cotton fields. She had long, strong fingers, and a back that never broke in spite of.

When I was born the mills had been shut for many years and she was older, worn down thin. Her smile was lost to a flat line she wore morning into night. Then I was born into this earth knowing she walked in beauty. I brought out the light in her. She rocked me, fed me, kept me and remembered how to smile. In silence we sat content side-by-side and watched a gas flame flicker, heat the room, keep the ice of age and loves hurt haunting outside where it belonged.

To Estelle I was a precious story still unfolding. She marveled in the magic of my being. I was a different kind of love that arrived unexpected. We both bore the melding of our generations with a simple adoration.

Still I was a child yet growing. To live and search for my first true loves and she, a woman growing older in the waiting for one true love to find her. And, rocking there on a given day, she looked out and made her fast decision.

She left him. A brave step after fifty years that rocked the boat, shook up all the old traditions. In a rush of love at seventy she remarried. Dyed her hair blonde, and got a curl. The new husband of her choice and keeping bought her dresses, earrings, flowers. They held hands in their sleeping.

All that pain of early on, all that hunger, all that mean of him—then love and righteous living. A different style of man who smiled every time she walked into a room. It bears repeating—every time.

Maybe in the end it had been worth the wait of those fifty years of crying. Maybe in the end this true there had been perfect timing. Because surely that end outweighed the past. She grew younger in his arms. This fact there was no denying. And, this new man loved her to the end as strong as their first day's meeting. You would've said so if you had seen them.

A stitch-painted wordmap that I see of Estelle from memory.

Her standing tall under the broad old oaks. She looks older than her years in the midst of this scattering of graves. There's no rhyme to their planting. A large stone here, a small one there. No order to this keeping. The tombstones shout and whisper, here lies a poor man's lot. Tiny babies born to die too soon under winter skies.

Her marriage ran that old road that offered promise of escape. Lead to a dead-end wood. A tricky ditch. A dark despair. A life of ash and recompense. In one old photograph, she is there, black and white standing by a broken fence leaning against a winter sky, mere shadow beneath a skeleton of clouds, so tired of propping up her world.

The bones of her very soul sick with dry and dirty lies. Estelle now worn to ice, to root, to earth, to death. But all the while her heart held hidden chambers with silent promise keeping. Chambers meant for love not even this one could discover.

Bones worn clean to root, to cold, to truth. But true love's death—no, it be not coming.

Hold still. Silent. Shhhh. Hush now. Hush, hush now and listen.

A shifting move, a something twining. A sleep unslept. A new made wake. A seeding, shuffle, sure forth coming.

Wake, wake. Wake and Listen.

The silent shift of seeding root to broken heart. Seasons of alone to love again. A deep, drunk green that is spring rising once again from the South. A promised pulse.

Let me be, she says. *Gone to dead dry husk, can't you see?*

But seeded rooted is seeded be. It rises from the marrow bone. From chambered dark of heart. Rises from the floor of soul.

Look here, God, she says. *Weary eyes done closed to that kind of good. Closed to romance in this life.*

But still. There is a flash of flutter. The first rise of night. The begin again of new.

What impossible new grace is this, she asks.

Bone turned to flesh, heart turned to warm. This rise again, this begin again. What miracle is this new love? This old to young again? Death's last kiss as sweet as first. Evergreen and keeping.

∽

My mother was the baby child but born old soul. As time went on she kept Estelle safe from Earth's cold wind. Tried to keep her safe from all ill will. Built her a little house. Not so much but roofed and warmed. Tried to help her be not wanting.

My mother (we call her Queen), a smaller woman than Estelle in stature but not of heart. There resided that same strength but this one screamed survival.

At two, death came knocking at her door, a disease of poor man's plight. Her all defiant soul met death at the door with nails turned black and fought to remain among the living. Again, the Queen in cotton field when appendix ruptured. Rushed to a doctor who brought the blade and the bottle. They had to take her in the night to find yet another doctor who was upright and sober. Still she lived again to fight.

Years later as I stood and watched. A bleeding ulcer made its silent weakness known. A late night life-flight. The doctor only speaking German, iced her body as they tried to keep her among the living. She slipped them into realms beyond the living but remembering me, my sister only three months living, she rose from the grave, her heart re-beating. Came home to us.

And still, a car crash in the night turned our worlds inside out. Yet, in all illogic she survived this.

Death came, but the Queen, the begetting egg of me, spit death out and wiped her mouth with daring.

This is her story.

⁓

The Queen

Bring it, death, she says. She's not quite two. A poor girl laid out to die all dressed in white. Nails gone to black from plague unknown.

But dying doesn't take. She rises. Eats. Drinks. Remains.

At fifteen planting in empty fields under scorch of day an appendix ruptures. They found her in the dirt dying there beneath the sun. Miles from help, they took her still in hurried hope.

The doctor, whiskey drunk, started cutting, but he was pulled away. To be or not to be—her life was weighed. Decision made, they rushed her yet again for miles and almost too late an ether curtain fell, silenced all her screams, the cut-away began. She lived but the scar became a legend.

At thirty with a new born babe, she fell to silent crashing. White, ashen, blood drained dry from a silent ulcer. She was gone then for sure. Helicopters carried her to Nuremburg. Doctors speaking rapture as she slipped away. But this one root, to me, to sister, pulled her from that dark dream, she forced her heart to beat again. She finally came back to us searching close our faces, where we had grown and shifted in her absence waiting.

At forty-two the queen is hurled up and out of crashing steel. Spiraling, bumping, shredding across three hundred feet of asphalt. She lay there silent, still, eyes opened to a darkened sky as flashing red drew nearer. A paramedic, brand new with shaking hands whispered, *My God, this woman's still alive,* just before she closed her eyes. Death, inside the door now, smiled, its fingers cold and clinging to her mind that fought back against death's dark whispered, *you shall be nevermore.* One silver ray of light, the ache of day. The pain of living. Home again. Risen from this damned grave, she carries on. Limping but alive, death once more defied.

But the character of death, hungry ever after, comes reaping yet again in silence.

At eighty, cancer climbing up and 'round the secret places eats at flesh and swears to seal out her life for once and all, but cut and bruised and cursed, the Queen whispers, *Death be damned, this round belongs to me.*

Keeping humor, fear abating, radiation takes the stage, doctors waiting.

She turns her mind and heart like flint to death and doing so, she goes on living. Holding court, telling stories from back ages, she rocks great-grandbabies to shush their fears, to whisper, *I've won the fight and little child, you are the bone of me. Remember that when death comes calling.*

Still living, the Queen reigns deliciously, defiant.

∽

River

What to say for this gypsy soul of mine? It's easier I think to toss a joke, to share a laugh over bourbon or a beer. Let's swap stories far and wide and talk of anything but me. I'd rather not, you see. It's been a hard, cold winter of six some years. Damned disturbing, truth be told. I thought I'd made it finally to a simple life. To have and hold. To trust a love that found me wanting.

How very dangerous this thing is we consider being human. I hate it, love it so. It breaks my heart in more than a hundred thousand pieces. But better this broken prism friend than a colorless existence. This fire of me—inside it smolders, burns and blazes.

I walk a broken path where past is fact of what once was. The best, the worst—it all depends on who you're asking. As tired as Estelle by that Winter fence, as tired as Mother bleeding.

But this blood running through my veins, this DNA of Estelle and of her daughter, I carry them and carry on. Deep seed to root.

This is the word story of my dark season. Of a continued journey yet unknown but calling.

∽

Me

Shadowed winds bare my soul, split it wide open. My heart's dreams are full-on dying. Shattered shivers, glass to sky. How dark this grave of where I've lived loving true while inside all is dying where pain runs deep where love's so shallow.

Gone are a lover's whispers, now only lies remaining. My heart, still hot to touch, is scorched from this burden of trust believing. A scar has sprouted, grown so quick, so thick, so tough—it casts a shadow and wields a shield from loving.

Heart locked sure then welded shut to sun and shadow both.

Life, j*ust let me be. I want nothing from you but silence.*

Yet, here is this grandchild pushing through my broken silence. A certain love that trust can't break, a constant love abiding. I know this place, have once possessed this place of grace, sitting close against Estelle's shadow. Now, I rock, give thanks for one who knows my beauty bubbles from my soul, that spring that is everlasting.

And this desire I have, something so close to death, to die to love at least and avoid the hurt that death ushers in turns me to face that royal state where the Queen looks in surprising. What made her so defiant? What made her will to stand again, to dare to be, to reach for survival lasting? Then I realize it was for me, this will to live, to see me peaceful, full of laughter. To know that us, those she leaves behind, are well and living life at its full force, resilient and abiding.

Fine then I think, for the young ones, and the old, the Queen herself, I'll rise again but not without a shadow. Let that other love, the one of story, quest, and conquer lie silent like Estelle's grave. Its time has come and gone, and what didn't last can turn to ash hereafter.

Yet, passion's purpose still runs deep. Refuses to be denied. With just one moment's glance, one full moon, one tree branch sketched large against the night-skies dawn surprises. This blood rushes up and desire rises to the top of skin and sinew.

The warmth of morning sun shifts the seed of hope, stirs and frightens me awake in ways once locked away in silent scar. Awake to crave a lover's kiss that is life, found both in true friendship and adventures waiting.

The band plays on; the song still finds me moved with tune and timbre. And I shall dance with all my might fueled by Estelle's strength, forged with the Queen's determination. The passion of my gypsy soul set free with resurrection.

III

Blooming in Place

❧

The purpose of life, after all, is to live it, to taste experience to the utmost, to reach out eagerly and without fear for newer and richer experience. —Eleanor Roosevelt

A Couple Bad Nights in Brindisi

Nina Gaby

People say that Orion is called Orion because Orion was a hunter and the constellation looks like a hunter with a club and a bow and arrow. But this is really silly because it's just stars and you could join up the dots in any way you wanted.
—Mark Haddon, *The Curious Incident of the Dog at Midnight*

It was well after midnight, many years ago. I sat against the door of the *pensione* in Brindisi in the heel of Italy's boot, with my own boot heels wedged tightly against the opposite wall in the narrow hallway of Room Three. Two men were banging on the door with their fists. Each bang reverberated against my spine until they finally lightened and the voices and the noises moved away, down the steps towards the concierge desk. The concierge was of no assistance. He was one of the men banging on my door. It was certainly the kind of night that can change a person.

I clutched my Swiss Army knife as if it was an amulet, as if it could really be of any help, and scooted across the floor to my backpack to dig out the emergency bottle of Courvoisier that friends gave me for my trip. "Just in case." It was a silly gift, a little sample bottle, just enough to coat any experience that may need momentary lubrication. This was certainly that time.

The silence downstairs was now scarier than the noise. I opened the knife and wondered how close the vital organs are to the surface and if the length of the blade could reach anything significant. Just in case.

The syrupy liqueur slid down my throat. It was the closest thing to safe that I had at the time. I thought about home and how I ended up on this hotel floor. I didn't even pretend to think that I knew about safe. I stared at the menacingly blue pea coat left on the chair and felt its damp stink from across the room.

"Night is the blotting paper for many sorrows–author unknown" I had scrawled in my journal while still on the train across Italy. Leaving my home in America weeks before, the "lover"—that's what we called them then, whether they loved us or not—had given me this knife wrapped in a note that said, "open many a happy bottle with this." As if he wasn't even sorry I was going. Not even trying to persuade me not to go. Giving me a knife with its choice of openers to feed my addiction. He didn't even think about it protecting me. Never even considered the blade.

If the door broke, I figured I could ram the thing into one of the guy's sides and at least get the liver. A heart under its cage of bone would be impossible. But I couldn't remember which side the liver is on. There was no more noise downstairs anyway. I threw the knife at the coat, locked myself in the bathroom, and took a shower that cost me an insulting few lira to operate if I chose hot water. It was a long time ago. Today there would be no lira. And certainly no Swiss Army knife, new regulations being what they are.

Grappling with artistic success and romantic failure, against an incessant soundtrack of Bob Dylan's *Blood on the Tracks,* I had decided, "Well, I'll just go away. *That'll* show him!" I thought of that decision as I stood there in that cramped green bathroom with the harsh light bulb illuminating every rust stain, every mold spore, every pubic hair from the last occupant of that worn out *pensione,* wondering if they too had been washing off the grit of midnight in Brindisi. Washing off the body memory of close calls, I thought about how I wanted authenticity. I wasn't yet aware that life is more layered than linear. I wanted to find a poetic way, a clearer straight line through the darkness that Dylan could sing about but my art was not reaching. What I wanted was different than what I needed. I needed to escape.

I think of a moment only months before, bleak and sleepless, when I lifted my hung-over head off the littered worktable in my studio and began to plan a trip that would include a freighter across the Mediterranean. In January. What could be a more authentic statement than that? I was as much in love with the image of myself invincible and alone as I was with the man I was leaving. I would give myself a year to wallow.

A handful of people suggested that I might be more afraid of artistic success than I was acknowledging, but my therapist thought the trip was a great idea. This was the same therapist who saw nothing wrong with all this drinking or any of the myriad excesses I brought to the couch every week. (The same therapist whom I would challenge a year later, when I was determined to stop drinking and this therapist extolled the virtues of mere moderation, a deadly idea in vogue at the time.) There was more to all this than just a fucked up relationship.

Mid-snowstorm, the night before I left home, my "lover" and I lay on his futon. The candlelight's flickering wasn't about romance. He had refused to pay his electric bill. Probably not refused, probably used the money for something more pleasurable, something he could ill afford. Somewhere in the rational part of my brain I knew that such a lack of responsibility, which had held a sense of novelty for me, would pale in its intrigue and one day disgust me.

∽

Even in my later and very secular sobriety I argued the idea of "higher power." I argued that we are fundamentally responsible for our own decisions, our own fates. But surely something was dragging me down the street away from him that night. He never did ask me to stay, nor would I have considered it. For reasons unknown to me then, I had prepaid my departure, in full, allowing fate's considerations to be stalled.

Long after, I found out that this man became infected from IV drug use, a part of his life that I hadn't known about. Blood on his tracks? How did I never notice? Higher power indeed, I eventually acknowledged.

⊷

Jamming a chair under the knob of the *pensione* door as I had seen done in movies, I picked up the knife again and got into my bed, the irony of his gift not escaping me. The knife was still shiny and new. I held it open in my hand and woke up in the morning with it still there, my muscles aching. I had not moved. The pale Mediterranean sun of this particularly harsh winter flowed in past the shades I had not closed, leaving them open with the windows unlocked in case I had to jump out.

There were morning hotel noises and smells coming from downstairs. Everything seemed so normal, another morning in Italy.

I had started my trip by flying to England, staying for a month in a London flat with some friends from art school. From there I took a series of trains across Europe and had a series of typical adventures of the ubiquitous sort for the American woman traveling alone. Upgrades, they would be called now. *Head of the line, Mademoiselle?*

I was offered coffees and drinks wherever I went, which I refused politely. A night train conductor through France offered me first class privileges in trade for other privileges. I laughed him off. I did not feel flattered. This was not flattering. It was something else entirely. Men followed me through Venice and

Florence as I tried to find quiet places to sketch and write and look at art. They watched me pay homage to Juliet under her balcony. I stopped making any eye contact. They quietly climbed the steps of the towers behind me and ambushed me from behind the mosaics. They tracked me across piazzas and into cafes. I finally stopped ignoring and started telling them loudly to "fuck off" as I fingered the Swiss Army knife in my jeans pocket. I had been traveling alone since I was eighteen and there really wasn't anything that I couldn't handle. And what I couldn't handle, in retrospect, I chalked up to Life Experiences that were buried, riches I hoped would value with age.

My last train stopped at the end of the line. Stormy Brindisi at midnight. I was excited to get off the train and onto my boat, the *SS Livorno*, crawl into a bunk, and sway through the Adriatic to the Mediterranean to Haifa, where I had lived years before. It would be like home again.

Youth and pride obscured any true fear or longing. Five days at sea. Stormy, January sea.

But the storms had sent the *Livorno* along without stopping in Brindisi. It was on its way without me. The dock was empty.

A hand grabbed my shoulder. A youngish man tried to explain that he was from the shipping company. "I am here to say the apology. For the boat. Is gone." He wore a navy blue pea coat and a knit watch cap. He looked as though he could be involved somehow with a boat. His skin was ruddy and rough. We had difficulty conversing.

I had learned no Italian, and was in a hurry to get out of Italy. There were once romantic notions in my soul, of course. Flings with dark, exciting Italian men. Heated whispers over an espresso, urgent bottles of cheap red wine, and then off to make passionate *amore* somewhere with balcony windows flung wide and a Fellini moon smiling through diaphanous curtains. Even the thought of this had become embarrassing.

As he held open the door of a tiny, battered Fiat, the pea-coated man was explaining that he was sent to help me find a place to stay until morning. The shipping company would pay. For dinner, too. OK, I said. What else was I going to do?

We drove for a few minutes, reaching what I remember in the wet darkness to be a chartreuse stucco building with a lit sign that read, simply, "*Pensione.*" The young man hoisted my back-pack inside and at the counter he spoke rapidly with the night receptionist, the "concierge," a vacant man with an uneven fringe of dull black hair creating an asymmetric slash over his brow. I felt his sleepy scrutiny as he nodded to the ruddy man's staccato sentences. "Okay, okay" was all I understood. They moved my pack next to the stairs.

"You want eat something? Drink something? The company pay," offered my driver. The thought of going out for some wine was appealing.

"I'd rather walk if you don't mind," I said, making little scissor movements with my index and middle finger as I declined getting back into his car. He paused, hand on the car door. "Okay, okay. We go over there. It's okay." His gaze lingered a moment too long. But I was thirsty and there was an open restaurant down the road that I could see from where we were standing.

The wine tasted good and I nibbled at some pasta as my companion kept telling me to "Eat, eat...the company paying." He interacted cheerfully with the waiter, a little too boisterous and chatty. I found the candlelight playing off his pockmarked skin disturbing, his unwashed hair just one more affront to my fantasy. But I was mellowed with train lag and alcohol, tired at last. I told him I was going back to the *pensione*. I was fine to walk by myself but he insisted that he come with me. It was easier to let him than to argue. He tried to take my hand as we walked back. I gently tugged away and smiled politely. I was almost back to the hotel where I could just shower off several days of train and worry about all this in the morning.

He followed me into the lobby. Despite the hour, the wine, the travel, I remained eager with the anticipation of getting to my room as I kept telling him "*Gracias, graci*, okay…good night! I need to sleep. Thank you so much!" The receptionist became alert. He stared at us over the "*Concierge*" sign, my backpack still on the floor by the stairs where we left it. When they begin to speak to each other I could understand only "*tre*." Three.

"I help you," said my companion, with more authority than I had heard in his voice before. The concierge's eyes did not waver. "No, it's okay, really, I've got it." I answered.

"No," said my ruddy companion, stooping to pick up my pack and growing ruddier. "I will take it."

The concierge again said, "*Tre*."

We just stood there. I sensed an impatience. *Okay, I breathed to myself. Okay. I get it.*

✥

"*Gracias*," I mustered as brightly as I was able. I was very wide awake then, very sober. As my companion began to lug the pack up the stairs, I struck up a conversation with the concierge. Wildly digging for any syllable that even resembled Italian. Anything that would allow me to stay down here and look stupid. I did not want them to know that I was not that stupid. I wanted them to think I was so innocent that I could not even imagine what they had in store for me.

I was boring the concierge. This scared me more than anything. There was no human desire here, just something that at first I didn't understand. Then an ancient knowledge descended.

My companion for the evening called out from upstairs. The concierge answered him. I could not understand anything. I kept talking to the concierge. Babbling. I asked him the time. I told him about Juliet's balcony in Verona. I tried some of my high school French on him. I pretended to flirt a little. Just a little. Just enough to pique the interest of my companion who came down the stairs to investigate. Maybe she is enjoying this? I wanted them to think that this would be easy. Relax, buddies. A sure thing. An American woman traveling alone. What could be better?

Easy now, I said to myself. *Easy.*

With a great shove I pushed my companion off the bottom step, hard, and I flew, flew as I never imagined I could and never will again, up the stairs and into Room Three where my back-pack had been placed next to the bed and the navy pea coat was tossed on a chair and I slammed the door and turned the lock and threw myself against the flimsy plywood.

Suddenly my angry companions knew enough English to call me a bitch and a liar and a cunt with "*putan*" thrown in for good measure. I wiggled one finger into my jeans pocket so I could pull out the bottle opener-slash-knife without moving away from the door. I stared at a bit of my reflection in the shiny blade and reminded myself not to romanticize this moment. The knife was not intended for protection. The knife was intended to keep me in a space of dependence. Would I return to the lover and America in the same shape I left?

❦

Almost. I came back from the trip much earlier than intended, not making the full year I had allowed myself. My younger sister was getting married, a time considered hard on confused, alcoholic, and unmarried older sisters. In a weakened moment at the time of my return, I found myself for a moment, just a brief *not even a kiss* moment, back on the futon. As if nothing had happened. As if there had been no victory. While I sat wedged on the *pensione* floor, of course, I could not foresee this. I had no idea of the victories to follow.

⁓

Finally, other guests awoke and pounded on their walls, and soon the hallway became quiet. I took my shower and managed a few hours of sleep and in the morning found out from a German woman having a coffee in the breakfast room that two days ago the body of an American woman was found in a ditch nearby. They still didn't know who she was. Her passport had been stolen. They knew she was American because of the Levis twisted around her ankles.

By the time I got to the shipping office of the *SS Livorno* to report what happened, fear had become an ill-managed state of indignation. I was taken quickly aback when the travel clerk assured me politely that no representative of his company had come to meet the train.

"So who was that guy?" I asked. The guy whose filthy pea coat was still in my room.

"I cannot imagine who that might be," the shipping clerk said with a shrug. His English was impeccable. He told me proudly that he had studied in England. That, in fact, his wife was British.

"How the hell does she stand it here?" I burst. He smiled patiently. He told me I was very lucky. It is a dangerous town at night. Especially for a woman as beautiful as myself. I told him to cut it out. He laughed and stamped a plane ticket as "paid" with a flourish.

"You can get out of here tomorrow. You will fly first to Rome and then to your beautiful Tel Aviv. 'Hill of spring,' yes?"

He bought me an espresso next door, quickly apologized again for the *SS Livorno*'s rerouting, and assured me the night concierge at the *pensione* would be fired. He had no idea who the other man was but would find out. "I am pretty well known in this town," he boasted. "What almost happened to you was terrible, a true embarrassment." He wished me a *bon voyage* from that point on. I relaxed, thanked him, and returned to the *pensione* to lock myself in my room for the rest of the day and night until I took the commuter plane to Rome at dawn and then, finally, to Israel where I spoke the language and knew all the tricks.

I had picked up some cheese and a couple bottles of wine, kicked off my boots, and gotten into bed. It was a late afternoon light through the windows when I woke up to the phone ringing. "A phone call for you, *Senora*," said the voice of a female operator. "Okay okay. Put it through. *Graci*."

No one in the entire world knows where I am, I thought, except for last night's companions and, of course, the travel clerk. The impeccable voice on the other line was smooth, conspiratorial. Stirrings of the Fellini moon and the curtains blowing coursed wistfully through my sleepiness.

"I want to see how are you...I mean how you are."

Very cute, I think. Almost. "Why are you calling me?" I demand.

"Only out of concern, of course. Only because you had such a disturbing time in our town, because of my company failing you."

Of course, I think. *Sure. Sure thing. Such a comforting voice.* He was much more what I had imagined when I imagined Italy. But still. Still.

"Shouldn't you be going home to dinner about now? To your British wife?" He has not yet suggested anything, but it's there, lurking in the lilt of his perfectly toned voice.

"No, not yet. I feel it is much more important that I show you that all Italian men are not bastards."

"You want to show me how Italian men really are, is that it?" I am sounding as neutral as possible given the circumstances. I am drunk and still very tired. The Swiss Army knife is open to the corkscrew. A line from *Blood on the Tracks* insinuates itself into my thoughts as Dylan describes pain as "a corkscrew to the heart."

"You want to prove something to me," I say.

"Yes. Oh yes. May I come over? To the *pensione*? We can talk about it."

A corkscrew to your head, I thought. *A fucking goddam twelve-inch corkscrew to your head.* But I didn't say it. He was one of only three people in the entire world who knew where I was.

I finished the second bottle of wine. I didn't know what lay ahead, this night or ever. Those were the kinds of nights that can change a person.

᷉

Addendum

Now, thirty-eight years since that night "that changed a person," I sometimes long for the me that existed before that shift. There was a wildness, a rawness. The woman I have become has cultivated a compulsive seriousness. An unrelenting need to achieve. Each moment defensively considered—how will it stack up against the next?—protecting whatever time remains. The force of the wind, higher power or whatever, that pushed me towards Brindisi pushes me still but under a variety of different intoxicants.

Some might say the real story here is in the recovery from alcohol. Some might say it's a "coming out." That I broke bad habits to find that the human heart, under its cage of bone, will do anything to free itself. Feminist, activist, separatist, and the subsequent realization that who I was meant to be was the person most carefully authentic in the moment. Alcohol lurked, waiting to lubricate any slide backward. Instead of AA I swam laps. One lap, two laps, then the seventy-two laps that made the mile I swam six days a week. I would say it was mostly about diligence.

I went back to school. I became the therapist I myself could have used, an advanced practice psych nurse, and now I spend my very serious life treating people with addictions and mental illness. I have taught at university. I have had my artwork in important places. I write essays. I've won awards. I've been married to one good man for the past twenty-eight years. I have a daughter who is almost the age I was when I landed on the *pensione* floor in Brindisi. She does not know this story. She became a hard worker, an ardent feminist quite on her own. She drinks a bit too much for my liking.

A life with many layers.

Recently I was in New York City to do a reading of an essay that took some courage to write. The morning after the reading I wanted to go to the apartment of a man who is a foremost expert in *boro,* the valued antique Japanese textiles I have become obsessed with. I wanted to meet this man, possibly set up a phone interview for the future as I research my next book idea.

❧

Scared of the subway and a heat so oppressive my heart was tick-tocking like an old Timex, this woman—the me who was once unafraid to go to the middle of the roiling Mediterranean—

couldn't seem to get herself to Greenpoint, Brooklyn, despite careful directions and a phone number to call. The friend I was staying with in New York, a friend with whom I was once raw and wild, fretted that I would get lost. On the phone my husband was too busy to hear my worrisome regrets about the woman I used to be, that woman I now cherish the memory of, who planned her escape across the Mediterranean in a stormy January. He hears that all the time now—*who I was, what I was.*

It may seem an inconsequential end to this essay, but I went, and I got lost, found, redirected. The fabric expert and I spent the morning talking about scraps of old cloth. The *boro*, stitched together centuries ago, by necessity, by candlelight, by hands nearly too cold to hold the carved bone needles. We talked about how the problem of keeping warm in the brutal northern Japan winters, on land too rocky to grow fibrous plants for cloth or graze sheep for wool, was solved by taking every scrap of worn fabric and patching, patching, layering, reusing the old thread. About how the accidental patterns rival even the most skilled abstract art. About how the women knew exactly who they were supposed to be.

When Dusk Fell an Hour Earlier

Beth Ann Fennelly

I was rolling jeans into tubular bundles and tucking them into my suitcase, packing for Prague. This trip would be the longest that I'd been away from the kids, and also the farthest.

"Don't worry about us," my husband said.

"Okay," I said.

"We'll be fine," he continued, sensing my anxiety. He handed me an ingot of clean socks. "And what a cool opportunity, returning at age forty-two to the country where you lived at twenty-one. Talk about closure."

When I left the Silesia, on the Czech-Polish border, I never imagined it would take me so long to return. But after I flew home to Chicago, I loaded up the car and drove 55 South to Fayetteville, Arkansas, where I entered a graduate program in creative writing. I met Tommy the first day. I'd told him about Prague's beauty, and we'd hoped to travel there, but first we had no money, and then we had no time, and then we started producing small humans. But I wanted to stand once more on Charles Bridge. Begun in 1357, spanning the Vltava, its stone parapets are topped with baroque statues of saints. To the right, through the arch of the gothic tower where coronation parades pass, lies cobblestoned Old Town. On the left bank, Malá Strana rises to the Prague Castle. The view, all 360 degrees, is wondrous, and nothing diminishes it. Not the night, when twinkling boats slide beneath the barrel-vault arches and the castle is golden, uplit; not the early morning fog that magnifies the church bells; not the impressionist rain that clears pedestrians and christens pigeons; not the mute snow that epaulettes the shoulders of the saints.

"Have you decided what to do for the long weekend?" he asked.

Between the two five-day workshops I was teaching, I'd be free. "Well, Berlin is a short train ride from Prague. Or Krakow. Or Budapest."

"I thought you were thinking of revisiting that border town where you lived? Didn't you write a letter to somebody there?"

"Yeah, my old office mate. She invited me to stay with her."

"Then why wouldn't you go?"

Only because it was the site of my failure. Only because it was the loneliest place on earth. Only because, when I lived there, I was disliked—abstractly and impersonally—by almost everyone I met.

～

I've always been jealous of those who came of age in the sixties or seventies. My adolescence overlapped the gross and greedy eighties, Reaganomics and trickledown and *The Preppy Handbook*. Dan Quayle misspelled "potato" on national TV. Rodney King was beaten by the LA Police, who were acquitted, and the riots that followed killed fifty-three, injured two thousand. I yearned for poetry, for justice, for revolution. Then, in college, revolution at last began, first in Poland, then Hungary, then cascading through the communist bloc. Finally, I was living through history I could thrill to. I taped this cover of *Time* to my freshman dorm room: joyous college students in jeans, boosting each other to the top of the graffitied Berlin Wall. The headline read "Freedom." In Czechoslovakia, a persecuted poet-philosopher-playwright had inspired student protesters, and the Velvet Revolution played out on the world stage. A rapt audience member, I watched as Prague, in the following months, filled with artists and seekers, drawn by cafés and cobblestones and cheap rent and oodles of jobs teaching the lingua franca. Why not join them?

Perhaps you've heard Prague described as "the Left Bank of the nineties." When I would take the seven-hour train trip there, I spotted Left-Bank-worthy expats, scribbling in notebooks at the English-language bookstore, drinking pilsner at the English-language bar, hooking up at the expat disco. They were bohemians, in Bohemia. Golden Prague, the city was called.

The Black Triangle: that's where I lived—depressed, industrial Silesia. Part of Nazi Germany in World War II, Silesia was returned to Czechoslovakia in 1945. Before that it had various borders and national affiliations—it had been an early Polish state, then part of the Hapsburg Monarchy, then Prussian before becoming German. In coal-mining Silesia, talk of freedom was met with skepticism.

Yet even for Praguers, it was a heady, disorienting, vertiginous time. Shortly before I arrived, hair dye did, but just one hue, a purplish-brownish maroon. Overnight, it seemed, Czech women dyed their hair to match their livers. The first fashion magazines arrived. The first billboards hawked goods—Sony stereos, Cartier watches, BMWs—never before available; now available yet unaffordable. Crime increased. Prostitution. Graffiti. Neon. Real estate agencies. The Gap. As the nineties rolled on, Americans in their twenties with large ambitions and little capital opened Mexican, Cajun, and barbeque joints. But where young Americans saw free market, many Czechs saw free fall. Under communism, there'd been no unemployment. The government provided a job, although it might be handing out single squares of toilet paper in restrooms. Or chiseling coal from an underground seam so hazardous that my local (still communist-leaning) paper listed miners dying at forty—of "natural causes."

When I arrived in August of '93, I'd never taught before. Like most "teachers" flocking to Eastern Europe, my sole qualification was that I spoke English. The arrogance in that stance wouldn't reveal itself until later. Yet, while I made countless mistakes, I possessed a surfeit of enthusiasm, so rare a commodity that I think my students worked hard simply to trigger it. So, ultimately, it wasn't the teaching that broke me. Nor was it the fact that I moved to a region with no English speakers while speaking approximately zero words of Czech. I learned Czech, in that way you learn if you want to do little things, like, say, eat. Potatoes, cabbage, garlic, and onions—these terms were on quick rotation, for typically those were the sole vegetables. At the market or at the nationalized stores, waited on by a clerk, I'd order two of something, or five, because I couldn't pronounce the dreaded "ř," a sound unique to Czech, found in the words "three" and "four."

No, it wasn't the teaching or the language. It's that I failed to be liked. Before I left the U.S., I'd told people I'd be "immersing" myself in Czech culture. My part, I assumed, would be showing up. Oh, it would be hard to find a girl more naive than the one I'd been, stepping down onto Czech soil with my Notre Dame diploma and "We Are the World" theme song and the conviction, which had never failed before, that folks would like me if I smiled hard and tried hard, both skills I'd perfected. Yes, I was a very smiling, very trying girl.

As part of my contract, the college loaned me an apartment in a twelve-story panelák, built of pre-fabricated, pre-stressed concrete panels. A large grid of paneláks was called an "estate"— gray towers endlessly replicated, as if in some apocalyptic mirror. Each panelák was partitioned into identical small apartments. Václav Havel called them "undignified rabbit pens," but his metaphor fails to capture the soul-crushing uniformity. Over a million of these apartments were built between the 1960s and

1980s, stretching the length of the country; they still house one-third of the Czechs. They were cheap to build, and the thin walls allowed the trusty warden—each building had one—to monitor his neighbors. The flats' lack of individuality was designed to foster a collectivist nature, but conversely made residents secretive, yearning for privacy.

Enter one do-gooder American, lingering in the foyer, hoping to make friends. Probably my neighbors assumed I was a spy. I spent my days in silence: I'd rise from bed, sometimes leaving behind on the pillow my head outlined in coal dust. I'd walk to the business college, teach, then walk home under sooty skies, dark at 4:30—dusk fell on average one hour earlier in the Black Triangle than in the rest of the country. I'd hunch through my "estate" (I can't seem to write that word without scare quotes) to my absurdly ugly building. I'd climb the cement stairs, exchanging the stink of burning coal—diesel-mixed-with-single-malt— for that of cooked cabbage. If I passed a neighbor taking out the dog, he or she answered my "Dobry den," but that was it. Inside my small flat, cheap beige industrial furniture stood on a cheap beige linoleum floor. From my toilet, I could hear couples above and below arguing.

I was the first American most of them had seen. I became a symbol: because the Czechs couldn't pronounce the "th" consonant cluster in my name, they called me, simply, Američanka — "American woman"— pronounced "Amer-a-CHAUNK-a." When I shared this ugly sobriquet with a friend in Amsterdam, he sent a postcard addressed to "Američanka, Silesia." It reached me. It took three months, but it reached me. I imagined it forwarded from town to town—Silesia is 1,700 square miles— scrutinized at each for a secret message in the dim postal light.

The Czechs were studying me, perplexed, and I was studying them, perplexed. I had questions, but no one to ask. For example: where were all the men? And I wasn't thinking about hotties—just men, period. Karviná, my city, was supposed to be 60,000 people, though it felt like much fewer. The shops and streets were occupied by women. Men were found mostly in the pubs (which seemed to be *all* male). Later, I would realize where the men were—beneath me, literally, in the mines. And I finally understood another thing: why the men wore eyeliner. Coal dust had painted the crevices of their eyes. They worked eighteen-hour shifts, three thousand feet below the surface. The mineshaft elevator took seven minutes to belch them into the world of light. They'd shower, then trudge to a dim pub and drink, some-times passing out right on the sidewalk after closing time. Walk-ing to school in the morning, I'd step over their legs.

I had no computer, of course—it would be a year before that strange term, the "World Wide Web," would be bandied about—and no phone (there was one at the University, on which I called home once a month). What did I do with myself? I stud-ied Czech, trying to master the damn "ř" (a trilled "r" pro-nounced *at the same time* as the "zuh" of "measure." Go ahead, try. See? You can't do it either.) I wrote letters, mostly to my soon-to-be-ex-boyfriend in Scotland. ("Dear Colin, I haven't gotten many letters from you lately. In fact, none. Which isn't very many.") I filled notebooks with maudlin poetry. I tried to learn English well enough to teach it. I dreamt of lettuce. I spent weekends so silently that sometimes, greeting my class Monday, my voice snagged in my windpipe. And I read the same dozen novels over and over. A typical evening: I finished *War and Peace*, rose from the chair to make tea. While it steeped, I peered down from my window to the dumpsters, because I liked to watch the Romani ("gypsies," I was warned, "all thieves"). They wore bright colors and babies strapped to their backs and if they found something good in the trash they called out gleefully. I wrung out my teabag for reuse. (Living in a poor country taught me thrift. I'd brought three ziplock bags, and I'd wash and hang them to dry. I still feel a pang when pitching a ziplock.) Then I'd return to the one chair, pick up *War and Peace*, turn to the first page, and begin again.

I was twenty-one, and fun, and pretty, and it didn't seem fair.

When I couldn't take it anymore, I'd send an "Expres" postcard—it cost extra but took just three days—to one of my two English teacher friends, announcing that I would visit. Kathleen and Elaine, an American and a Canadian, were each stationed in lovely, ancient cities, and rooming with other English speakers, which is to say, they weren't nearly so crazy-ass desperate. With those kamarádkas, I saw a good bit of the country, and we never failed to have an adventure. Once a bitter, blond waitress in České Budějovice triple-charged us for our smažený sýr— breaded fried cheese, basically a mozzarella stick on steroids— thinking we were dumb Americans who didn't know better. But we were even dumber than she thought: to punish her for extortion, we dashed out the back door without paying. Which Blondinka had anticipated—she was hiding behind the dumpster. In defeat, we handed over the money. But spiteful Blondinka secreted the money and called the cops anyway, who apprehended us at our hotel. I can't imagine we were hard to find. Only some *very* sweet talking kept us from getting deported.

Laughter. We laughed a lot, but looking back now, I identify an edge to it. We smirked at Czech thrift, even as we practiced it. We—I think it's fair to say—condescended. We traded our students' malapropisms and language errors. (My favorite, harvested from a love letter—the student wrote that I'd given his heart "the fire," but, because I'd rebuffed him, now I gave him "the heart burn.") We ranked tacky window displays, arranged by descendants of the original owners who'd had their stores stripped from them. Now, due to restitution, the stores were returned to the families, who might have nothing to sell or no talent for selling. (My favorite window: a used wedding dress surrounded by used car parts.) We joked about babičkas, matrons between sixty and ninety, short, square, with droopy brown dresses, woolen cardigans, knee socks, and heavy-bottomed shoes. They hawked loogies the size of beanbags and, when the bus pulled at last to the stop, elbowed anybody in their way.

None of this is making me sound like a very nice person. You're not a nice person if, buoyed by idealism, you move to a country to help it and end up poking fun at it whenever two or more are gathered in the name of English. But I couldn't seem to help myself. And the release was short-lived. Too soon, I'd be riding the last Sunday train. Looking out the window, I could tell I neared Silesia when the buildings leaned. The coal mines had so honeycombed the earth that the topsoil had settled, called "subsidence." Even the ground is depressed here, I'd think.

I'd never understood the privilege of living with beauty until I lived in a place bereft of it—in food, in architecture, in aesthetics, in nature. I'd never even *considered* the privilege of living in environments that hadn't harmed me. Now, sometimes the tap water was brown. Bottled water was more expensive than beer. I drank a hell of a lot of beer. I've always been a runner, but when I tried running in Karviná, people stopped to watch. They'd actually *point* at me. With actual fingers. I couldn't bear it. Furthermore, back from a run, I'd cough a black scum onto my palm. It seemed healthier not to exercise. Instead, I ate smažený sýr, putting the "CHAUNK" in Američanka.

As the months wore on, sometimes a group of students invited me for a beer. And my colleagues—Hedvica, who'd once taken a course in England, and Kristýna, Head of Languages and Head of Liver-colored Hair—were cordial. My office mate, Ẑdenka, was more than cordial. She invited me to hear jazz a few times across the border—jazz, which the communists had suppressed because it celebrates individual improvisation.

Ẑdenka had long brown hippie hair with blunt bangs. She was a natural polyglot, her English probably better than mine. When she was a girl, her sixteen-year-old sister fled Czechoslovakia for France. Ever since, Ẑdenka's family had been persecuted. They were watched. They had files. Likely their apartment was bugged. Young Ẑdenka's pen pals in Switzerland and England stopped writing—later she'd realize their letters had been confiscated. Ẑdenka's brothers in the army (there was a mandatory conscription) received the worst assignments, the lowest pensions. Her mother's applications for a bigger apartment were rejected. Because of Ẑdenka's English, the officials suspected that she, too, would flee. So this woman who spoke five languages had, each year, her request to take a trip abroad rejected.

Ẑdenka could have been my friend. And she was, in her fashion, but cautiously. Halfway through my year, we were in our tiny office—our chair backs almost touching—when I opened a letter from my father. My dog had died. "He was a dog among dogs," wrote my emotionally reserved father. I started weeping, feeling so damn lonesome and cut off, tears plopping fatly on my father's expensive stationery. I thought—Why doesn't she put her arms around me? What would that cost her? My self-pity ratcheted up my sobs—a real drag-your-palm-across-your-snotty-nose-boo-hooing.

Well, who knows how much hugging me would have cost her. Decades under totalitarianism had cored even the best of them.

Did I think about bailing? I did. Sometimes, on Thursday evenings, crossing into Poland where I taught Conversation at a high school, I'd think about all the other borders I could cross. But I'd signed a one-year contract. I made it to Christmas, anticipating a trip to Greece with Kathleen. We'd go by bus, a long, long ride, but as we were paid like Czechs—thirty dollars a month—we'd travel like Czechs, our backpacks stuffed with food. In Slovakia, however, the bus pulled over and the driver strode back to our seats, yelling for us to produce Yugoslav visas. It was the first we'd heard about any such visa. Maybe he was angling for a bribe, which wouldn't have been unusual. Either way, visa or bribe, we didn't have it. He dragged our backpacks down the aisle, then hoisted them out the door, into a gutter filled with dirty slush.

Next: two girls, six days, no money, no moderation. In a Bratislava pool hall called Mamut, we played challengers for beer and entered some never-before-and-never-again zone of skill and sass. Toward dawn, our competitors having fallen away, Kathleen walked to the fingerpost sign in the corner that pointed to various cities. She tapped "Vienna, seventy-five km." A look passed between us, then we were turtling our backpacks onto an eastbound train where, for the next seventy-five km, we dodged the ticket collector. We certainly couldn't afford to drink in the Viennese beer hall where we wound up a few hours later, but when a huge table of huge drunk Austrians began cheering soccer, we picked up their chant: "Go, Leo!" They were delighted— Leo had fans in America! "Cheers to Leo!" boomed Kathleen, and they raised their glistening steins. "Ah," she emoted, incredulous, despondent, raising her hands in the kind of big gesture you use when talking to drunk foreigners, "but we have no beer!" Rectified. Every time we got thirsty, we felt moved to make another toast.

It was either that night or the next when we scored beds at a convent, with real live nuns in wimples, all very *Sound of Music*. And we ended our trip in Salzburg, where, on the eve of the Lord's birth, a kindly pastry cart owner gave us free apple strudel, saying almost shyly, "Merry Christmas." (There hasn't been, and will not be, a superior strudel. That was the Ur-strudel.) We decided to head back to the Czech Republic, as we'd been invited to Christmas dinner with Kathleen's student, so the next morning before dawn we hitchhiked to the station in the back of a newspaper delivery van, hurling papers out the double doors into puffy falling snow. We made it in time to join the student's family for the traditional Christmas carp. To ensure freshness, the Czechs keep the live carp in the bathtub until the feast. My clearest memory of Christmas 1993 is huddling with a nice Czech family in their tiny bathroom as the patriarch hammered a fish.

So. I didn't make it to Greece, but I'd made it through Christmas, and now to spring with the promise of my mom coming to visit. The weather warmed, and when I woke, I rarely saw my head outlined on the pillow.

There was no thawing with my neighbors in the panelák, though. One sleepless night I lay wondering what Karviná must have looked like before socialist-realist architecture. Probably the same nineteenth-century plaster-walled buildings that lined the square had been here, I figured, but demolished to clear room for my "estate." Then something so terrible rushed into my head that I sat up and grabbed it.

The people who'd lived here, whose houses had been demolished: they'd been Jews.

Kathleen and I had visited Auschwitz. We'd gotten there via bus from Krakow, so the journey had taken several hours, but not long after, a map showed Auschwitz only forty miles away.

I'd seen no Jews in this city of 60,000 people, no synagogues, no Hebrew writing.

So that was the other reason this place was poisoned. It wasn't just coal pollution. It was ashes.

Before I left, I experienced one last alienation, this time from my conscience: I went to bed with a student. It was mid-April, the night I'd learned Kurt Cobain had, a week prior, committed suicide. I could tell you my student was only one year younger than I was, and that lots of expats were engaging in this type of extracurricular activity, but even at the time—indeed, even as he unbuttoned my blouse and lifted my lonesome breasts and lowered his mouth to them—I was aware it was wrong. My teaching was the sole thing I'd been proud of that year. No longer. In class Monday morning, I looked at my students, and I knew that they knew. We reviewed restrictive and nonrestrictive commas.

Finally, it was time to pack. I junked sheaves of overwrought poems. I gave away my exhausted, beloved books and my exhausted, detested clothing. I triple-ziplocked a stub of cheese before pitching it, imagining the Romani pulling it from the dumpster with a shout.

My colleagues organized a farewell reception, bread and sausage and mustard and pickles. They presented me with a manicure set. If you press the latch, the velvet case pops open, revealing several sharp little instruments all hugged to the suede lining with elastic tabs. It would have cost them a lot of money, even divided several ways, and I was surprised by it.

I left with less than I'd brought. And a good bit less certain about myself and the world than when I'd arrived.

Now, at forty-two, I'd return to the land where I lived when I was twenty-one. My friend said, "You must feel like Rip Van Winkle." But Rip woke in a body that had matured with a spirit that hadn't. My spirit had aged with the rest of me. I'd gotten over being disliked by an entire nation: I'd met Tommy. One shouldn't underestimate love. It can make you a more generous person. Also, the concept of loneliness had been declawed. I used to pity solo female diners; now, sometimes, cutting my sons' meat, I envy them.

And I'd gained perspective. One frustration of my Czech year was living with so many questions. (I never did learn whether my "estate" was on the former Jewish quarter. Whom could I have asked?) I had no newspapers, no analysis. Now I better understand the pressures warping the culture. For example, in the 1970s and '80s, according to Amnesty International, the secret police "carried out more than 230 executions, jailed about 280,000 people on political charges, and confined about 7,000 people in mental hospitals against their will." Everyone knew the police relied on spies and informants to get dirt on dissidents, but few knew the extent of this network. Until Lustration. Lustration—"clarification through light and fire"—began in 1992 when former dissident Petr Cibulka published the names of 160,000 alleged informants. Over breakfast, Czechs opened the newspaper and found names they'd suspected and perhaps, in addition, friends, lovers, or siblings. Some informants had been manipulated, blackmailed, or tortured into collaborating. Some merely wanted a job transfer or a two-week travel pass to France. Either way, Lustration, still simmering when I arrived, did a number on my neighbors' eagerness to invite the new girl in 6B for slivovice.

Another thing I'd come to understand is that history is never as absolute as it's portrayed. Looking back, we see '89 as a decisive end to forty-one years of communism. We use the word "revolution." The Silesians used the word "change." Their mood was a tad more "wait-and-see." The lamp posts in Karviná still held the megaphones that, a few years earlier, had blared speeches and martial music across the square. The statues of Lenin and Klement Gottwald—the first Worker-President—had simply been carted behind the police station and laid on their sides. They seemed dozing, resting up for a regime change.

That long-ago *Time* cover I'd taped to my dorm room— "Freedom!" with college kids dismantling the Berlin Wall—

captured an honest euphoria. But euphoria was just one honest response, and the most photogenic one.

After I'd returned to Chicago in '94, my Czech year grew very distant very quickly. Less accessible, less referenced. More Mylar-wrapped. I kept up with my two kamarádkas, of course, but they both moved on to other countries. No Czechs came to visit me. I never met anyone who'd been to Silesia. Never heard it mentioned on the news. My house isn't filled with Silesian souvenirs. I rarely hear Czech. I studied two other languages, which put Czech a few rotations back on the mental rolodex. Ẑdenka and I exchanged Christmas cards. That's about it. That, and the fact that I still dreamt about that land. Sometimes, opening my eyes in the cool, clean Ozark morning, I'd expect coal dust on my pillow.

At Arkansas, I was surrounded by native speakers of poetry. My tribe: I'd found my tribe. I got help with my writing and improved. Now I've published a handful of books, and I get some nice invitations, but I'd be lying if I didn't confess that I was pumped to be offered a paid gig in Prague. Lying if I didn't confess that, when I landed in July 2013 in the airport renamed for Václav Havel, I squelched the strut of the dork-in-high-school-returning-to-the-twentieth-reunion.

And, though I expected it, as I taxied to my hotel and later explored the city, I was gobsmacked to see how Prague had changed. McDonald's and malls and cineplexes and Internet cafes and T-shirt shops and technopop. Bob Dylan had played the night before. I ate a salad. I ate a fruit smoothie. I ate at an Indian vegetarian restaurant. All this was kind of trippy—I kept enduring the disorientation one gets waking in a strange hotel—and all this was expensive. Not because I was triple-charged, either. Or, more accurately, because everyone is triple-charged now.

One thing hasn't changed. Charles Bridge is still stunning, despite the scrums of tourists, some on segways, clustered around the stalls of souvenirs lining the bridge. Behind the stalls, the Japanese brides and grooms lean against the parapets with their iPhones on selfie sticks so they can fit the castle in their photo. Yet, somehow, Golden Prague is still golden.

Oh, and the beer is still delicious. Now I had someone to drink it with: my friendly American students. They invited me backpacking to Budapest over the long weekend, which would have been less freighted, less discomfiting, than being the house-guest of Ẑdenka and her husband Petr, essentially strangers now. They'd feel they needed to entertain me, and I'd be dependent without a car. But I was curious. And returning to Silesia felt like something I should do.

I took the (newer, faster, cleaner) train, and as it pulled into Karviná I recognized Ẑdenka—her hippy hair had grayed. I stepped onto the platform and we hugged, the most natural thing in the world. I gave Ẑdenka a bouquet I'd picked up in Prague, and Petr carried my duffel to their car. They drove me to a new restaurant with an outdoor beer garden, tables shaded by oaks. For old time's sake I ordered smaẑený sýr and ate the hell out of it while Ẑdenka took photos with her giant camera, and although I normally don't love a lens in my face, and certainly don't love it while I'm yanking strings of melted cheese into my craw, I was bemused by her documentation. I felt a palm on my shoulder and turned to find a smiling, elderly woman.

"We thought we'd never see you again," the stranger said.

Hedvica. It was Hedvica. Ẑdenka, I learned, had planned a gathering of my former colleagues.

Hedvica took a spot across from me. "May I request a favor?" she asked. "Would you remove your sunglasses, so that I might better see your face?"

When I did, she smiled. "You quite look the same." She handed me notes from two former colleagues—Kristўna, caring for her "ailing mum," and Vlasta, with her new grandchild at their country chata. But the colleagues who were in town joined our table and began reminiscing, an unsettling experience in which I was a character I didn't recognize, so discordant were their memories with my own.

"Don't you remember your nickname?" one asked.

"Yes," I sighed. I still hated it. "Američanka."

They laughed. "Oh, yes, that's right." They laughed again. It was funny to them. "But don't you know your other nickname?"

I shook my head slowly.

"Ah. We called you 'Sunny Chicago.'"

Sunny Chicago? We were speaking English, but I felt lost. They'd had this adorable nickname for me? Sunny Chicago? Really?

The conversation moved forward, but I did not. I wanted to whine, "Why didn't you call me that in my hearing?" I wanted to demand of Ždenka, "Why didn't you hug me while I wept over my dog?" But it's not just that these questions were ridiculous, petulant. It's that they seemed to come from a time that had never existed, that had no logical tie to any of us here at this table, where sun rippled through the leaves overhead and dowsed our group with an underwatery glow.

My colleagues, leaning in, were speaking in low voices about Jiři. He remembered me so fondly, they said. How sad, what happened. They shook their heads. He'd had a drinking problem, you recall, vodka, and he starting missing classes, and was found passed out under his desk. They fired him on the spot. So sad. Died a few months later. He would have loved to have been here.

I didn't even remember Jiři. I cast back for his face and nothing swam to me.

For half my life I'd thought of this place, these people, as chilly. But who was the chilly one now? Karviná did feel freighted, but for different reasons than I'd predicted.

The waiter went by and I asked him—flotsam Czech seemed to surface when I grasped—to tally for me the bill that is kept on the table. But the paper on which he'd recorded the slash marks had already been whisked away. "You're too late," he said, nodding at my colleagues.

Afterwards, Ẑdenka and Petr drove me to their house and showed me the room where I'd sleep. The nightstand was lined with a dozen framed photos. Even from the doorway, I recognized them: my yearly Christmas cards. The faces of my children.

The rest of the weekend passed in outings overlaid with a troubled nostalgia, correcting and corrected. Ẑdenka was a conscientious hostess, eager to show me the spots I would remember. I'd subtract the renovations and try to imagine myself into the scene. That outdoor market—minus the whitewash, minus the bright trays of strawberries and arugula, if given a sour, yeasty odor and a few bins of geriatric potatoes—might have been, yes, had been the market I haunted, ordering in twos and fives. I remembered the first time I'd spied carrots; someone else had nabbed them by the time I found *mrkev* in my dictionary.

When we strolled over to Poland for a coffee, I turned my head to follow a streak of red: a spandexed runner. At the border, the guardhouse appeared empty. I recalled the Thursdays when the guards would scrutinize my passport, the same guards who'd scrutinized it the Thursday before, eventually fisting a stamp beside the previous one, thrusting it back as if I'd gotten away with something. Now, I wondered if those guards had paged through my stamps not to inconvenience me, or not solely to inconvenience me, but because they were thinking of the countries they'd never see.

The main square of Karviná could have been the square of any small European city. It had always been desolate, half the stores boarded up—in a Western, cue the tumbleweed—but still a respite from the Soviet architecture surrounding it. Now the buildings had been scrubbed of soot. The blue umbrellas of outdoor cafés shaded families eating gelato, gentlemen with newspapers and a coffee or small beer. The fountain, formerly an empty shell, flung streamers of water that sparkled in the sun. In fact, there was sun. Only once did I smell burning coal. The scent seemed almost sweet.

On the corner of the square was a pharmacy, perhaps the same one where I'd once dropped my film off during that long winter. Nowadays, I sometimes tell the film story as an example of that culture of surveillance: when I'd gone back for the developed photos two weeks later, a group was bent over the counter—the male pharmacist and three women, discussing, pointing to something. As I waited, it dawned on me that the focus of their critique was my photos. They must have seen me, but they kept on, unhurried. I stood by, having no other choice, until they were done. But now I considered why those photos—which probably all featured Kathleen, Elaine, and I mugging in front of some Czech castle—would have interested those four Czechs. I imagined them looking at our smiles, our clean, white, fluoride-in-the-water, orthodontically straightened, North American chompers, the kind their daughters, who rarely smiled, would never have.

Ẑdenka had retired from the business college but asked Petr to drive us there on Sunday. I figured I'd look in on our old office, my classroom, and the mailroom where I'd waited for letters from Colin that never arrived, an acceptance to graduate school that did. When we got there, the cleaner-but-still-ugly building was closed. Ždenka knocked on the glass but couldn't summon a guard. "Don't worry," I told her. "I'm more interested in seeing my old panelák."

After Ždenka photographed me in front of the college, we crossed the parking lot, feeling the heat of the afternoon rise from the asphalt. I found the shortcut to my "estate." I set out with confidence on the dirt path and after a few turns spotted my building. But the potraviny shouldn't have been so close. I moved down the treeless walk to another panelák, thinking it was mine—but where were the dumpsters? I traversed another row, Ždenka switching her heavy camera bag to her other shoulder and revealing a bandolier of sweat, Petr blotting his face with a handkerchief. I turned left, and left again, scanning, then realized we were back where we'd started. Petr, switching to Czech, asked Ždenka if he could carry her bag, if she needed to rest.

"I'm sorry," I said for maybe the fourth time.

"It's okay," she said, smiling, solicitous. "It's important that you find it."

Was it? I didn't know anymore. I felt confused, and guilty, and confused at feeling guilty. I didn't want to extend this sweaty parade. Yet I didn't want her to feel that my comeback tour had been disappointing. Also, I didn't want to reveal that I couldn't identify my panelák, that I no longer remembered my place in their world. That I had never understood it from the start.

What was one more misinterpretation, at this point, one more way that I'd remember things differently, one more way that I'd be out of tune? I staged a cry—"Here it is!" and pointed to a panelák. Ždenka raised her camera to her eye.

There I am in the photo—still a very smiling, very trying girl.

That afternoon we said our goodbyes, and I took the train back to Prague, and in a week flew home to the arms of my beloveds. For the second time, I left that country a good bit less sure of myself and the world than when I'd arrived.

Closure: so satisfying. So tidy. But maybe overly tidy. Closure suggests an open question demanded an answer, and received one. But what happens when the questions change? Did I need to forgive the Czechs for not liking me, or did I need to forgive myself for not realizing they'd liked me as much as they'd dared? Forgive myself for being too young, too limited, for lacking the empathy to sufficiently imagine their world? And, if I managed all that forgiveness, what next? Should I go about revising how it felt to live there? That Mylar-wrapped story, the one that begins, *Once I lived in a place so polluted that dusk fell an hour earlier, once I was disliked by almost everyone I met*—do I rewrite it now that I've discovered the narrator was naive, unreliable?

The manicure set—a velvet case that springs open, all the sharp instruments in their elastic loops—I still use it. I wish I'd thought to mention that. I use it. I do.

Syringa Vulgaris

Alexis Paige

Common Purple Lilac: "A mass of medium-light purple blooms every year. A magnificent New England sight for nearly 400 years. When a nursery friend looked out John's living room window and thought he had some fancy new cultivar, he chuckled, 'Nope, just the good old common purple.' Never disappoints. Suckers freely, the best lilac for a spreading hedge. *Syringa vulgaris.*"
—Description from the Fedco Seed Catalog

"And the day came when the risk to remain tight in a bud was more painful than the risk it took to blossom."
—Elizabeth Appell

In my fortieth year, I appear, by most external measures, happy, stable, comfortable—even rooted. I have a kind, handsome husband, a burgeoning career, two inseparable dogs, and an old farmhouse on a riverside in Vermont. I don't mean to suggest this exterior sketch is false, but Emerson once remarked on the enormity of what lies within us, and therein, of course, lives the fuller picture. Beyond our Fisher Price town, with its steepled square and mix of Colonial and Victorian storefronts, lies a road that winds along a small river. Between this river and the road, farms nestle—some ramshackle, some picturesque—in the furry, coniferous hills of central Vermont. Down this road a few miles sits our first house, which Keith and I bought last summer, flanked on one side by hay fields and on the other by the not-so-mighty, but lovely, First Branch of the White River. A few miles past our house, the First Branch empties into the main branch of the White, which then empties into the larger Connecticut about thirty miles downstream. Because we lived in Arizona when I was a child, and swimming pools were ubiquitous, Mom plunked me in a toddler swim class at two, and I've been a water lover ever since. Given a chance to swim, especially in the wildness of an ocean, lake, or river, I will stay submerged for hours—until my skin is pruned. Here, in the town of just over 1,000 souls that we now call home, I watch and listen to the river daily from our back deck. If the weather is warm and the river high enough, I head down to the water for a dip or to sit on a giant granite boulder, deposited as glacial moraine during the last ice age, and marvel at my fortune. Something I can't yet name is washing over me here, or perhaps that something is finally washing away.

Nearly fifteen years ago, and 6,000 miles from the apartment in San Francisco where I lived in my twenties, I sat nervously in a cold, stone office in the bowels of the stazione policia, on Via Zara in Florence, Italy. I was twenty-five, and on my first trip abroad. The night before, I shared dinner with friends on the Piazza della Repubblica, fifteen minutes by foot from the police station. The night before, I wore an outfit I bought special for the trip: tight red pedal pushers and tight red blouse, heeled sandals, and purple headscarf. We chatted gaily with our waiter, who joined us for Fernet Branca and Prosecco after his shift. He spoke little English, and I little Italian, but with broken Spanish and flirty eye contact, we managed well enough. My friends and I and the waiter walked over the Ponte Vecchio, but at some point while browsing the trinket shops and smoking cigarettes with our arms draped through the stone portholes over the Arno, he and I drifted from the group. At another point, I figured my friends had gone back to our hotel, and he offered a "corto trayecto" on his moped. Still drunk and sunbaked from the day, intoxicated by the wafting lilac and street disinfectant, and dizzy from the ridges of terracotta rooflines undulating by, the ride exhilarated me in those first moments. But after twisting down more dusty lanes and bumping over cobblestones and emerging onto a faster, wider boulevard, my giddiness evaporated. I began to feel sick and to spin, adrift from my friends and our hotel and the center of town. He slowed the moped to a stop, hopped it onto a sidewalk in front of an apartment building, and with his strange, sweaty hand, the nice-seeming waiter led me up a flight of steps and into his small apartment.

ᷓ

We got here as soon as we could, my husband and I like to say—both in a literal and metaphorical sense—about our arrival in Vermont, about how we are late bloomers, about how long it's taken to arrive at some place we might call home. We came to Vermont eight years ago, fleeing Houston, Texas, in a little hatchback packed with everything we owned. We drove past the Texas refineries and Louisiana swamps, then into the lush hills of Mississippi and Alabama, and on through the Smoky Mountains and Shenandoah Valley. When we reached the Maryland panhandle, I knew the Mason-Dixon Line was close, and once over that arbitrary boundary, my body flooded with relief, as if I had been safely extracted from behind enemy lines.

I say that we fled because at the time, we felt that we had to get out of Texas if we wanted to make it. A few months before I met Keith, I got drunk and crashed my jeep into three other cars at a major city intersection. Miraculously, and despite epic vehicle wreckage, no one was killed, and only one person was hurt. After my initial arrest for drunk driving, I was charged with a felony that carried a five- to ten-year prison sentence, and the ensuing, protracted legal ordeal loomed over everything, including the beginning of my relationship with Keith. Dating tips don't cover how to handle the "I'm under felony indictment" conversation on the first date, but Keith stayed, even as life became going to court, going to AA meetings, riding my bicycle everywhere, signing up with temp agencies that would overlook my circumstances, reporting to pre-trial supervision twice a month, and finally, after almost two years in the system, enduring a five-day felony trial. I was fortunate in the end that the jury convicted me of a misdemeanor and sentenced me to just 121 days in the fearsome Harris County Jail. With good time, I served sixty.

My lawyer's early admonishment about the Texas criminal justice system proved prophetic: "You might beat the rap, but you won't beat the ride." While on the ride, Keith and I talked about "going home" once everything was over. Despite early years out West, I had spent most of my youth in New Hampshire, and on visits to New England Keith became enamored of the beauty, history, and landscape. He grew up in Texas, but as someone who is naturally taciturn, who loves flannel, snow, and early mornings, we joke that he must have been a New Englander in a past life. While I was in jail, and with a firm end date in hand, we finally began to make plans in earnest. Even though it was considered contraband, I kept a photograph stuck to my bunk with the adhesive strips from a stamp book, so that I could remember what waited for me on the outside. It was a picture of Keith and me, from the trip we made to Vermont for my thirtieth birthday, standing outside in an October snow flurry. Vermont had become our new starting line.

∽

Why did I go with the waiter? This was the tortuous refrain that ran through my mind the morning after, as I sat in the police station. I didn't speak Italian, but I found a sympathetic translator from the American Consulate who escorted me to the station to help me file a report. Why did I go? I thought, as she mouthed the Italian words for the images that stabbed into my mind as if from a knife. The words sounded cheerful when this nice lady spoke them in Italian, the words for *oral sex*, for *finger penetration*, for *erect penis*, for *without consent*, for *kick-start scooter*, for *champagne headache*, for *swarthy waiter*, for *slim build*, for a *Calabrian driver's license*, for *his e-mail address scrawled on a napkin*, for *No*, for a *partial apology in Spanish*, for a *cigarette afterward*, for a *walk over the only bridge in Florence to survive World War II*, for *permission to call my father*, for *the correct change in Liras*.

A movie about my twenties would begin happily. A young, quirky Ally Sheedy would star, Sofia Coppola would direct, and John Cusak would play most of my boyfriends. These early adult years weren't without bumbling and angst, but for the most part, I had my act together. I lived in my dream city, where I was on track to complete a master's program in creative writing. I had my own studio apartment on Russian Hill, a tight group of friends, and steady, lucrative work as a cocktail waitress, which helped me save up for my first European adventure. The itinerary dazzled me—Paris, Amsterdam, Switzerland, Italy, Provence, and finally, Spain—but I never made it past Florence. So despite the auspicious beginning of my fantasy movie, the film would end unhappily, would tumble perilously thereafter across the screen in a nonlinear montage of depression, substance abuse, and suicide attempts, or what one shrink euphemistically called "gestures." Not even the best film editor could suture these storylines. The jump cut was too rough.

This twist in my story has only recently, all these years later, begun to rise to a place from which I might access and write about it. It's the story of—and here's the problem—my rape? Or my sexual assault? The first term I associate, technically, with penile-vaginal penetration, and the latter with euphemism. None of what happened feels technical or easily categorized, and neither does it seem deserving of euphemism, a language akin to evasion. See how the words still confound me, how the taxonomy remains fraught? I suspect that when the writer becomes a statistic, the language has to be dealt with as much as the event. *Is rape what you want to call it?* my father said to me in those early days. Of course, he didn't mean harm. We don't learn how to talk about such things in our culture, least of all men, least of all middle-aged fathers whose daughters call from pay phones halfway around the world to say, *Daddy, I've been raped*. While I understand his quibbling now as an effort to make the thing somehow lesser or more manageable, or perhaps as an effort to attach language to the nightmare that we all could then live with, those words damaged me. I felt misunderstood and silenced, as if I couldn't be trusted to name my own experience. Though legal language varies, RAINN, the Rape, Abuse & Incest National Network, defines rape as "Penetration, no matter how slight, of the vagina or anus with any body part or object, or oral penetration by a sex organ of another person, without the consent of the victim." Even though, technically, my experience does fit the definition, the truth is that I remain ambivalent about whether to call what happened to me rape.

Not long after the incident, the translator stopped returning my e-mails. Over time, I got mail from the Italian court that I couldn't read. One letter came. Then maybe another. This timeline, too, is fuzzy, mired as these months were in heavy drinking and a growing dalliance with cocaine. When I returned from Italy, I holed up in my boyfriend Mike's nondescript apartment in the Outer Richmond, which in those years was still a working-class neighborhood on the northwestern corner of the San Francisco peninsula. His apartment was closer to my university and far away from my friends who lived downtown. Its location conscribed a small, anonymous circle of the city in which I could limit my travel and social activity. I felt safe only in the darkness of his apartment and zipped into the anesthesia provided by drinking. But the safety was an illusion, the alcohol and drugs provided only temporary relief, and, if anything, they slickened the slippery in-roads of my mind. Previously closed-off territory opened up, as if in a nightmarish version of Chutes and Ladders, wherein I replayed every slutty thing I'd ever done and every unpleasant encounter.

Long buried before, I suddenly remembered another assault, dredged from the depths of my consciousness like a car hauled from a riverbed, mud-caked and slick with algae. I was seventeen that time, and in my first week of college at Rutgers University in central New Jersey. Late in that first week, a junior from my dorm, a fast-talking, animated guy from Jersey City, took an interest. Now, of course, I know I should have been wary of a guy whose opening line to my roommate and me was, "Youse freshmen?" but then I was charmed. His accent and swagger were so different from the Boston Irish guys I grew up with, and he was not just some immature high school boy but a college student—a man. Within minutes he was showing me his Don Mattingly swing impression and inviting my roommate and me to his dorm room for movies later that night. We went, of course, and while my roommate made out with his roommate (another beefy guy from Jersey City) beneath the Under-the-Sea phantasmagoria created by a spinning lava lamp, he made a move on me. We kissed for a minute, but a hunger in his movements frightened me, and before long I demurred, asking him to "slow down." But he was somewhere else, his eyes glazed and fixed on the wall behind me. In fact, he sped up after I said that, as if further aroused, and then rolled on top of me.

"C'mon, baby," he grunted, grinding his erection into my thigh. I tried to push him off of me, but he wouldn't give.

"Please stop," I said shakily, looking over at my friend who seemed oblivious and tangled up with the roommate. I assumed happily so, but I have wondered since, what if she had been in trouble too? How could I know what I was seeing, having never been taught what to look for? He pulled my shirt up and took my breasts in his mouth, suckled hard and with his teeth, then cupped my crotch over my jeans, rubbing his thumb hard back and forth against the zipper, which is where I imagine that he imagined my clitoris was. Finally, I managed to wiggle free by shimmying up the bed and wriggling out from between his legs. I hopped off the bed, pulled my shirt down, grabbed my bag and shoes, and clutched them to my chest to hide my breasts, which were still loose from the bra that was now pulled around my shoulders like a sash. I hurried to the door with the man panting after me.

"Don't leave," he begged. "I promise I'll be good. You're just so sexy, baby." But once I was in the threshold of the door, he turned off the charm like a switch and snarled after me down the hallway, "Bitch." It's probably important to point out that Rutgers, a state school where most students' hometowns were no more than two hours away, was desolate on the weekends—an additional factor that made my roommate and me, two rubes from out of state, easy prey. As I rounded the corner to the freshman wing of the dorm, I heard him holler the charming words that my roommate and I later turned into a kind of revenge refrain: "You can't just leave me hanging! You gotta jerk me off or sumtin."

Mike worked long hours as an options trader, but I remember that one night he came home early with takeout. I couldn't tell you whether this happened six weeks or six months after the rape, nor whether it was meant as a gesture of kindness or normalcy, or even as a gesture at all, but his early return with dinner was unusual. Without much comment, I took a plate heaped with fried rice and egg rolls and my tumbler of White Russian and plunked down on the floor in front of the television in the living room. I had gained maybe fifteen pounds since the assault, and while I was nowhere near fat, neither was I the lithe ingénue he began dating years before. We were on the outs anyway, so what he said to me then—while not untrue—didn't penetrate my new armor. I was fortified by then, had taken up residence in my own sad kingdom. Standing in the doorway, his arms crossed, and with a mix of tenderness and perhaps disgust, he said, "Where is my bright, beautiful girl? I don't recognize you anymore."

I smiled wryly, raised my cocktail as in a toasting gesture, and said, "That, my love, is exactly the point."

I spent less and less time at my own apartment, which now seemed a place belonging to another person and time, a "before" shot from the "before and after" portrait of my own life. Through a bartender friend, I had lucked into the cute, cheap, centrally located rental. No one I knew paid $700 a month for a studio in the heart of the city, let alone one with a private garden patio that teemed with bougainvillea, lavender, rosemary, eucalyptus, and the purple Chinese houses that looked like ornate, amethyst bib necklaces. The elderly, housebound woman who lived upstairs had cultivated the garden for decades, but since she could no longer enjoy it, the garden became my private Eden—an idyll rich with a bracing cologne of eucalyptus and herbs. But that was before. After, I preferred exile.

No one seemed to want to talk about the assault anyway, or no one knew what to say, but perhaps that characterization isn't fair—or even accurate. Memorably, someone did say something—just the right thing, in fact. In a handwritten note on delicate ivory stationery, Jenna, a motorcycle-riding, beer-drinking girlfriend originally from Down East Maine, wrote, "You are the purest little rosebud, just beginning to flower. Please don't let this stop your petals from opening to the sun. Remember, in the end it is harsh pruning and bullshit that makes the rosebush grow strong." Perhaps I convinced myself that it was easier for everyone else, when I actually meant that it was easier for me, to forget the whole thing. After all, it happened a continent away, in another language even. The more time passed, the fuzzier and more distant the details became. Occasionally I would pull out the Italian paperwork from a file box. Four documents summarize my sexual assault: a report made by my friends; an initial filing made by me at a mobile police unit; a complete report made to the Florence Police; and a notification I received from the court many months later, and which, as far as I can make out, gave me twenty days to declare a domicile in Italy. I can read Spanish, and the languages are close, but still the documents are hard to decipher. I thought over the years about getting someone to translate them for me, but again it seemed easier to let it lie, to let the words, and therefore the event, remain a kind of secret or mystery that I kept even from myself. In a sense, then, I answered my father's rhetorical question about what to call it by default, by deciding not to call *it* anything, to put the whole thing in an unlabeled box and bury it on some godforsaken alien continent inside me.

≪

Why did I go? I hate that I still ask myself this. I know this what-if game leads only to self-blame and shame, but I play anyway, because this is what sexual assault victims do. Perhaps I shouldn't have worn red, shouldn't have flirted, and shouldn't have asked where we could get some pot. But actually, it was my girlfriend's boyfriend who asked, and the waiter who said he had some in his apartment. He said his apartment was just around the corner, and we could ride over there on his moped. He seemed so nice, so harmless. I should never have gone, should have said "no" more forcefully, should have kicked his teeth in—*something*. But what magical thing would I have done? I play this game, as all victims do, because our culture trains us to blame ourselves. Instead of teaching boys and men not to rape, we teach girls and women the dubious art of avoiding rape, and yet when, inevitably, women are raped, they are abandoned, or worse, they are revictimized by a legal system that reinforces its own bogus mythology. Every case becomes her word against his, despite empirical research that puts false reports as low as with any other violent crime. After mustering the courage to report these crimes in the first place, victims fight again to convince police, prosecutors, judges and juries, when ultimately, ninety-seven percent of rapists receive no punishment at all (RAINN). The message is clear: victims must bear their own burdens. We must learn how to survive our own rapes.

Though many of the direct memories of my assault remain sealed in drums, and buried like radioactive waste or time capsules under hard-pack, I am still not safe from them. Trauma interacts with memory in complex ways, so memories of certain events—flashes—appear to me as nonlinear images and sensory details. I am not unique in this. In an article for *Time Magazine* (December 9, 2014) on the neurobiology of sexual assault, Drs. James Hopper and David Lisak explain why rape and trauma survivors have fragmented and incomplete memories of their traumas:

> In states of high stress, fear, or terror like combat and sexual assault, the prefrontal cortex is impaired—sometimes even effectively shut down—by a surge of stress chemicals. Most of us have probably had the experience of being suddenly confronted by an emergency, one that demands some kind of clear thinking, and finding that precisely when we need our brain to work at its best, it seems to become bogged down and unresponsive. When the executive center of the brain goes offline, we are less able to willfully control what we pay attention to, less able to make sense of what we are experiencing, and therefore less able to recall our experience in an orderly way.
>
> Inevitably, at some point during a traumatic experience, fear kicks in. When it does, it is no longer the prefrontal cortex running the show, but the brain's fear circuitry—specially the amygdala. Once the fear circuitry takes over, it—not the prefrontal cortex—controls where attention goes. It could be the sound of incoming mortars or the cold facial expression of a predatory rapist or the grip of his hand on one's neck. Or, the fear circuitry can direct attention away from the horrible sensations of sexual assault by focusing attention on otherwise meaningless details. Either way, what gets attention tends to be fragmentary sensations, not the many different elements of the unfolding assault. And what gets attention is what is most likely to get encoded into memory. ("Why Rape")

Not only are the memories fragmented, but again because of the nature of trauma, and despite my best efforts to neutralize them, the memories intrude on my thoughts without warning. One moment I am sitting by my river at home, and the next I am back in Florence, holding my friend Bernadette's hand, then tap-dancing on cobblestone, eating pasta, on the back of a moped. Suddenly, the man's fingers are inside me. His tongue inside me. I am crying. His penis is in my mouth; is that right? I am crying in his kitchen, asking for a ride to the hotel. Then I am back with my friends, outside the hotel, in relative safety under some streetlights. Bernadette and I are having a cigarette, and I am racing to tell her before the man gets back on his moped. As I tell her the story, the man is apologizing, inexplicably, to Bernadette's boyfriend. *Where's my apology?* I want to scream. I am still waiting.

Perhaps because I am just now unearthing my sexual assault, it doesn't occur to me until all these years later, when my husband points it out, that this game, as I've always thought of the obsessive event replay, is a textbook hallmark of post-traumatic stress disorder. One morning not long after moving into the house, we are out on our deck, drinking coffee and admiring the view of surrounding mountains, meadows, and the river. The lilacs, which light up with pleasure the same brain circuitry that alights with fear—the amygdala—are still in bloom, and the river is running high. Listening to the rush of the water, I tell Keith about the compulsion I have to replay the night over and over.

"You know what that is, right?" he asks. I shake my head, even as I guess that I do. "It's PTSD," he says. I do it with the car accident too, another trauma. I'd always assumed that, because in both instances I was drunk, the replay was more about getting the narrative straight, trying to fill in certain holes. Is the inability to fill in the holes trauma, alcohol, memory, or all of the above? I run the replays automatically, absently, while drifting off to sleep or walking the dogs or washing the dishes. Each starts as a kind of mental video game, with Player 1 (me) flashing on the screen, and then we're off. Either we're running the crash scenario in Houston, or we're running the moped scenario in

Florence, each a sort of gauntlet where I imagine I can get points if I can lock certain features in place. Perhaps I can grab a new street name, a new weapon, or a new clue. Invariably, of course, the features of the game blur. So too with the features of memory, which escape me, bringing me once again upon the giant sinkholes that open up and swallow time, matter, memory, me.

"Lex," Keith says, waving his hand in front of my face the way we do to inquire if the other person is paying attention. And with that I come to, having been belched from the beast of my past, returning to our morning in progress.

"I don't know what's worse," I say. "The sudden jerks into the past, or the fact that I can never seem to stay in the present." I try then to settle into my chair, my body, my breath. "Be where your hands are," my yoga teacher says. I study my hands, my oversized mug, and the lilacs in the yard, so purple they are almost blue. With their heart-shaped leaves and from the way they cluster into crown-like bunches, they remind me of the swim bonnets worn by the elderly women at my fitness center. But the fragrance is so unique that it reminds me of nothing but itself.

High on adrenaline and instinct and a lifelong good sense of direction, the morning after my assault, I led the officers back to the man's apartment, which was not just around the corner as the man had suggested, but rather some four-plus back-switching miles from the piazza. Since I had the napkin with his name and e-mail address, the officers matched it with one of the occupants listed in their records. "Ben fatto!" one of the officers shouted and pumped his fist from the front seat of the little police car.

"It means good job," the translator said.

"I know," I said. While still parked in front of the apartment, the officer craned around to face me in the back seat. He began talking intently, passionately, and looking back and forth between the translator and me.

"He says he's very sorry this happened to you, and this is good evidence, but these things are hard to prosecute," she said. I nodded and thanked him. He turned forward as if to drive off, but twirled back again, this time addressing mainly the translator. I made out the last word, *comune,* common. I looked at the translator, and she shook her head.

"C'mon, tell me," I said.

"There's no precise equivalent in English." She sighed. "It doesn't mean quite the same thing, but he says these things happen. They are common."

When I packed for my flight just hours later, I flattened the words on the police report in the bottom of my suitcase like a freighted souvenir, underneath the red pants and blouse and stacked heels I wore the night before. I realized then that my panties were gone, probably still in the man's apartment. Once on the plane and headed back to California, my seatmate asked if I was going home, and I nodded, then faltered. "Well, yes, I live there," I said, thinking home was not a word I understood anymore, not a place on any map.

⟜

The night we closed on our house, Keith and I stood in the back yard at dusk with our hands clasped. We have two dogs, a nine-year-old rescue pit bull mix named Jazzy, and a one-year-old boxer puppy named George, whom we had gotten a year after our first boxer died. As a puppy, George, white- and fawn-colored with a comical black and brown eye patch of fur, is predictably mischievous, but it was Jazzy that afternoon who had gotten so excited upon visiting the house for the first time that she pooped in the entry way. We were still giggling about it as we stood in our new yard, watching George zoom around the acre in obsessive circles, which we call "racetracks." The river was high and the lilacs in bloom, and the music from the water and the perfume from the flowers washed over us. "This is ours," Keith said, squeezing my hand a little harder.

"Yep," I said, squeezing back.

The common purple lilac, or *syringa vulgaris*, like those in the loamy northwest corner of our own yard, is a flowering woody plant in the olive family. Olives thrive in temperate Mediterranean climates so unlike the harsh, snowy winters and humid summers of Vermont that it surprises me to learn this. I know it's greedy and provincial, but I've always associated lilacs with New England, which somehow made them mine. After all, the common purple lilac is the New Hampshire state flower, which I was forced to memorize in school, along with the state bird (purple finch), state fruit (pumpkin), state gem (smoky quartz), and state insect (ladybug). But I do remember lilacs in Italy, whose fragrance stood out to me amid the other Florentine scents—amber, tobacco, lavender, cypress—as a kind of olfactory beacon of home. The family name, *syringa*, comes from the Greek word syrinx, or hollow tube, which refers to the plant's shoots and their large piths, while the species name, *vulgaris*, means common or usual. However ubiquitous lilacs may be, nothing about their loveliness seems common to me.

Later that night, while washing dishes and looking out the kitchen window that overlooks a side yard where the previous owners had a sizeable fenced-in garden, I tell Keith about everything I want to plant. I am excited, and the list grows absurd: star fruit, melons, Christmas trees, cucumbers, potatoes, peonies, roses, bleeding hearts, corn, lilies, bananas, chips and salsa trees, puppy seeds, and book awards. Keith laughs. I've never been a gardener, never planted anything other than pain, but here in my fortieth year, I want to plant something finally that can thrive.

We've been in the house six months now, and while unpacking the last of the boxes, I find a package marked "fragile" in Keith's neat handwriting. I can't think of anything fragile we own—no valuables or heirlooms—but as I peel back the layers of plastic shopping bag used as wrapping, I see a box, about the size of a shoe box, which I recognize immediately as the urn containing the ashes of our first dog, Jimmy. A ninety-pound boxer, with a heart and personality to match his size, Jimmy came with us from Texas and lived here in Vermont until he was thirteen. Losing him was eased by the wonderful staff of our local vet office, who treated the loss as their own. We opted to have him cremated, and when we went to pick up the ashes, they were stored in a pine box with a handwritten card taped to the lid. The card, which had a raised, lumpy paper heart affixed to it, read, "Plant this in loving memory." The veterinary technician who emerged from the back to tell us how sorry she was explained that the heart adornment contained wildflower seeds and that we could plant it. At the time, we lived in an apartment and decided to hang on to the card until we found a place of our own. I show Keith the card and read the instructions out loud: "Remove adornment from card, plant in your garden, and wildflowers will blossom year after year." I ask him if he remembers the garden I was talking about our first night in the house. I hold up the card and touch the little heart adornment and say, "We can start with this."

Bibliography
"97 of Every 100 Rapists Receive No Punishment, RAINN Analysis Shows." RAINN, Rape, Abuse, and Incest National

Network. Accessed 23 November 2015. http://rainn.org/news-room/97-of-every-100-rapists-receive-no-punishment.html.

Hopper, James, and David Lisak. "Why Rape and Trauma Survivors Have Fragmented and Incomplete Memories." *Time*. 9 December 2014. http://time.com/3625414/rape-trauma-brain-memory.html.

Abuse

A Survivor's Message for the Vatican

Kim Michele Richardson

From *The Unbreakable Child,* Third Edition

I was deeply troubled when I read that Pope Benedict XVI was "weary and sad." I, too, am weary and sad. Let me explain. I've been answering calls, letters, and e-mails from countless victims of child abuse by the clergy for over a year now—calls, letters, and e-mails that the pope and the Catholic Church's hierarchy should be answering. So I thought I would send a polite reminder: apologies and accountability are due. I am a survivor of clergy abuse. Abandoned to a Catholic orphanage as an infant, for nearly a decade I was exposed to unspeakable abuses by Catholic nuns and a Catholic priest. It was only in the last year that these horrific abuses were publicly exposed that I was finally able to write about the long nightmare inflicted by those who hid behind His cloak to mask their evil deeds—deeds the Roman Catholic Church concealed while enabling decades of child abuse by predator clergy.

I wanted to forgive them and I did; however, I am often asked: How can you offer forgiveness to those who hide behind their righteousness, behind ill-conceived surety of their place in heaven and on Earth, those who have not asked for forgiveness because they do not think they need forgiveness?

Along with tens of thousands of victims globally, I am still waiting. We are waiting for an apology and an admission of accountability from the pope and the Church's hierarchy. We've waited, sometimes for decades. People like the CEO, also a former orphan and victim of clergy abuse, who has to lock himself in his office because he's having a "bad day." His "bad days" happen when the memories of physical and sexual abuse become too strong for him to function as a regular working adult. He writes to me hoping I can offer him strength, hoping I can make sense of crimes committed against him as a child that were the most heinous crimes committed in history.

Then there is the former priest who writes to tell me of rape by his "own." There's a nun, too. There is also the woman who suffers from crippling PTSD because of her abuses by clergy. She writes that she may not be contacting me for a while because she will probably be back in a "dark place" and will have to seek mental health institutional care for her "latest bout"—a bout directly caused by predator clergy. She prays she'll be strong and not be tempted again to commit suicide, as she's tried so many times before.

And before I forget, there's the strong advocate for victims of clergy abuse I've been privileged to know. He was not abused, but sadly, he is now "religiously empty," this man from a strongly connected religious background. I worry about him and his children.

There's also the daughter (one of five). Her mother, now deceased, a childhood resident of a Catholic orphanage, was severely abused and raped by clergy. The daughter says her mother's former clergy abuse touched everyone in her family and continues to cause trauma and discord so intense they have all sought counseling.

Pope Benedict XVI and the church's hierarchy have created a scatter bomb. Abuse. The abuse of one does not just stop with one; it also affects and harms their families, friends, coworkers, and society and on and on—so serious that it must be diffused.

To do this, the church must be willing to publicly help these deeply wounded, still-suffering victims and survivors. Start the cleansing by reaching out to us, answering and also disclosing the records of predator clergy that have been protected by the Roman Catholic Church for decades.

My name is Kim Michele Richardson. I am waiting, along with all those voices around me.

To you, dear Reader: Growing up in an orphanage for nearly a decade, and suffering unspeakable abuses, inspired me to write those reminiscences in my memoir, The Unbreakable Child. *I have been fortunate to have wonderful second and third and fourth chapters to my life. I am now enjoying a fulfilling life as a wife, mother, and full-time novelist and contributor to the* Huffington Post.

I am an advocate for the prevention of child abuse, working closely with survivors and law enforcement, and I have also partnered with the United States Navy to educate their global outreaches about the prevention of domestic violence.

Not everyone who starts out terrified and harmed is so lucky. One of my most cherished goals is that my story, The Unbreakable Child, *and the enclosed op-ed letter to the Pope I contributed to the* Huffington Post *will bring more awareness, provide hope, and kindle the hearts of people who have been victimized.*

IV

Blooming Again…and Again

I want to be recycled endlessly, and flower again
and yet again unexpectedly, bloom into
a surprising color for an old woman, ripe
with wrinkled youth and vigorous beauty,
with twinkling eyes in deep sockets,
making them wonder
just how I do it.

       —Victoria Millar (from "Credo")

Woman on a Half Shell

Wendy Reed

The Wharton College of Business has an online life expectancy quiz. There's a short and long version. But that is not the quiz that my husband and I took a few weeks ago. Ours dealt with odds of another kind: love.

It is Friday night and I have grilled some fish, which is to say my husband's stomach thinks it's been gypped. Agreeing to a healthy diet doesn't mean you won't miss the rib-eyes.

"Brain or body?" he asks.

It's a summary of question number six from "Modern Love" in the *New York Times*: "If you were able to live to the age of ninety and retain either the mind or body of a thirty-year-old for the last sixty years of your life, which would you want?" Even with its research data, the contemporary relationship quiz smacks of medieval love potions. While I'm contemplating this, the question has triggered my husband's worst fear: losing his mind.

He does not hesitate to answer: "Brain."

I, however, never hesitate to equivocate.

So I call into question the question. I cite methodological concerns. I rail against the profiling. I damn the culture of youth. I impugn the obviously shortsighted, oversimplifying authors, who ignore that some women by the time they are thirty have birthed three children enrolled in three different schools that play on three different ball teams at different parks, which pretty much means that by thirty, both mind and body are already shot. I also decry the measure of time and value, stoop to a "No brainer" pun, and cuss. But I do not answer the question. Instead, I wonder if my geneticist's findings should be factored in, especially with a name like Descartes, and I begin a tally of all the surgeries and procedures I've had since my husband and I met six years ago on Match.com.

As I talk, my husband's eyeballs begin to glaze over, but he does not say that the quiz was my idea and should take an hour—not per question but total. Nor does he remind me of how I'm always the one saying that intimacy requires vulnerability, not overthinking.

For that, I do not tell him that he's wearing two pair of glasses on top of his head. Even as he squints toward the clock on the microwave, I do not say a thing.

By the time we met, he and I had already logged four decades of matrimonial experience and so were institutional veterans who'd traded in their rose-colored glasses for bifocals. For us, online dating had been a way to find an enjoyable companion, an easy relationship—not marriage.

"I'm allergic," I'd said. "And I don't think there are shots yet."

But "Vernal Equiknox" intrigued me beyond his profile name pun (a nod to both the season of renewal and his grandfather "Papa Knox"), and because he was so easy to be with, I said yes when he proposed, even after he threw the ring at me. We were standing in my carport beside his truck, not sitting by the creek at the ranch he'd reserved. I apologized for ruining his romantic plans. He apologized for losing patience. I repeated with a laugh what Mother had told me all my life: "You could try the patience of Job." And it was true.

Then he laughed when I said he might be onto something with the ring toss thing. "I bet more women would line up to catch a ring than a bouquet."

From the beginning, "Worst foot forward" was my battle cry, and we'd both agreed to laugh at our warts, not hide them. It had seemed that easy. Never mind that our homes were separated by 120 miles and our offices by a three-hour commute. Hours of happy laughter turned into days, then months—just like that. *Easy!* was our decree. If two such wizened vets as we deemed it so, how could it be anything else?

❧

My husband looks at the quiz and clears his throat as if I might've forgotten about it. I can't tell if he thinks he's being subtle or not. I've learned many things from him, not the least of which is that someone who cut his teeth in the pits of Nascar and won the 4H tractor trials at the age of ten defines many things differently than I do, not just subtlety.

"You know both my grandmothers lived into their nineties," I say. He sort of nods.

Bigmama, even after decades of debilitating arthritis, still took the trash out into her nineties—albeit naked. Grandma Reed also had debilitating arthritis, but she worked crossword puzzles until her death at ninety-four, and, shortly after her ninetieth birthday, she fell out of a tree while shooting the dad-blamed crows for eating up her pecans. Because her hip healed faster than the thirty-something's repaired the same week, her orthopedist suspected Grandma of something tantamount to doping: use of a fountainous elixir.

But Grandma Reed, my sisters and I were fairly certain, had never drunk anything more questionable than her own well water and Tab—glass bottles, not cans. Nor had she ever set foot in St. Augustine, and the only way she would've come across Ponce de Leon would've been in a crossword puzzle.

The physician's suspicions were unfounded. But not lost on us.

So when one sister's diagnosis of rheumatoid arthritis preceded the other's sixty-fifth birthday, we figured a sisterly triage of fantastical proportions was in order. It was also a good excuse to visit my daughter and son-in-law, who live forty-five miles from the fountain of youth's mouth. So this past October, Daddy's "three Reed girls" headed south in my Mazda 3, our empty travel cups ready to be filled with miraculous waters. A couple hours in, we lowered the bar from search of miracle youth elixir to search of convenient toilets.

The day of the pilgrimage, my son-in-law recommended I rent a golf cart for easy navigation. St. Augustine is, we knew, the oldest city in the U.S., but my sisters balked. Old as their legs might be, they still worked. And I had to admit they had a point. But it's hard to dismiss the advice of a U.S. Naval Aviator with an engineering pedigree from Vanderbilt, who teaches something strategic that may or may not include classified weapons. It came down to the forecast: thunderstorms likely, with rain most of the day.

I paid with plastic and handed the golf cart keys to my daughter. Fountain of Youth, ho!

It turns out the ticket price of eternal hope is roughly the same as a margarita lunch, including tip. We Reeds are nothing if not cheap; and life in our family, no matter how long, is not worth living hungry. There is no cost, however, for taking selfies at the fountain's gates, which may be taken beneath the sign for as long as your arms hold out. Make of the gates what you will— fabricated as they are of iron and not pearl—but we cheesed it up and took our share

With as many pictures as we took, it would stand to reason that at least one would be good of all four of us, at least good enough to serve as an iconic souvenir. But gray hair is anything but reasonable. And although disguised by Miss Clairol's medium golden brown, it is still gray hair, which explodes in humidity. Even if there were words to describe what happened atop my head, I wouldn't use them.

"It's avant-garde," I explained to my sisters when they questioned why I cropped all the pictures down to our smiles. I then tried to cover my bullshit by waxing philosophical: "Smiles are not limited by constraints or time or the Tao of Now."

We'd ordered hamburgers to accompany our margaritas, but neither had arrived. I'd opened my photo stream because they wanted something to show for our journey, but apparently it wasn't empty cups and teeth.

At any moment the margaritas would arrive. I just had to bide my time and keep my phone out of their hands. So I took another tack and said, "Crooked and unbalanced as they are, our smiles reflect something about the ages." I intoned such passion that I was in danger of convincing myself. My daughter reminded us our ages were "Sixties, fifties, forties, and next month thirty."

"They reflect something alright," I heard one of them say, but I was halfway to the bathroom.

"I reckon it has something to do with our familial legacy being strong," I said when I returned. Admittedly the reckonings of an idealist can be simultaneously dangerous and cheesy. But that doesn't make them untrue. I am certain that my familial legacy, even if I can't feel it in my bones, is as undeniable as it is visible in our genetic lack of top lip that, despite cropping, lies right under my nose.

My husband never met my grandmothers. But both of his had careers in addition to their roles as wife, mother, and grandmother. His own mother's jobs ranged from switchboard operator at a hospital to running the local pool hall. He didn't, however, have sisters or cousins his age, just two brothers, so sexism didn't really occur to him until he had daughters. But marrying me came with historical discussions that questioned the presupposition of traditions, especially those that dehumanized and abused women. It also came with the offer that if name-changing had to happen, he could use mine. So he was not surprised when I stood in our own neighborhood beneath the sign that announced the new children's wiffle ball park and nearly blew a gasket because the only children represented were male. Nor did he shrug off my anger or diminish the implications of such female omission.

As the middle of three boys, he often played the role of peacemaker, and as an adult he confesses to being conflict-averse. Still he sends me articles like the hilarious one Alexandra Petri wrote for the *Washington Post*, "Famous quotes the way a woman would have to say them during a meeting," which includes:

> Mr. Gorbachev, tear down this wall!
> *Woman in a Meeting: I'm sorry, Mikhail, if I could? Didn't mean to cut you off there. Can we agree that this wall maybe isn't quite doing what it should be doing? Just looking at everything everyone's been saying, it seems like we could consider removing it. Possibly. I don't know, what does the room feel?*
>
> We hold these truths to be self-evident, that all men are created equal.
> *Woman at a Meeting: I'm sorry, it really feels to me like we're all equal, you know? I just feel really strongly on this.*

Although my husband's never had to alter his speech in this way, he's aware that it happens for women far more than most people realize.

"What does this neighborhood park sign say to our granddaughter? What is she supposed to think every time we stroll her by here?" I ask. "That only boys wear uniforms? That only boys play here? That girls didn't make the cut?"

He doesn't respond but keeps studying the sign.

"I can't just do *nothing*. I'm going to draw a girl."

"Why don't you put a girl's picture over one of the boys," he says. " One as high quality—or even higher— than the boys?"

That was three weeks, four days, and seven hours ago. Yet what I've done is nothing. What's the quote? All that is required for evil to flourish is that good women do nothing? (Let's sub "woman" for a while, since, as more than one man has said, "Get over it; it's just a word." Anyway, it makes more sense for "woman" to represent both men and women because only woman bears both; man bears neither.)

Because of me, evil is flourishing in my neighborhood. Although it's not female genital mutilation, sales of ten-year-old girls in the name of marriage, or death to girls who go to school, it is a social injustice, and this time I don't have the excuse of logistics, the cost of travel, or language barriers. It can't get any more convenient than right down the street.

All I need is a large image and some glue. So what's stopping me? Am I afraid?

I'm not afraid of the police. I've survived wrongful death charges, so vandalism by comparison would be a picnic. My problem, I think, is that I don't want to be *that woman*.

That woman, the mountain-out-of-molehill type; the "can't get over it" feminazi; the bitchy, man-hating shrew who harps on and on about inconsequential things; a too-serious Suzie who could use a good screw—or else has a loose one; an ill-bred inbreed without Southern manners; a femme fatale who ruins the party. *That Woman*, by the time Bill Clinton finished with it, bore additionally unfair but unmistakable baggage.

That Girl however was Anne Marie. Young. Charming. Innocent. And played by Marlo Thomas, a pioneering producer

147

who'd wanted to call the show "Miss Independence" and who stood firm in the face of history by declaring that a woman, and no one else, ought to define herself. The show aired the year I was born and is part of my earliest TV memories. It paved the way for *Mary Tyler Moore* and *Murphy Brown*, who were not wives or mothers or the help. These women were searching for—and unafraid of—their own power.

"That girl" came up on a return trip from the Louisiana Book Festival, where a friend and I had rescued books during a storm. We'd confessed to each other that we sometimes used the power pose to give ourselves a boost. Having waded through rising water in heels and a skirt, I was flush with adrenaline and feeling something akin to power as we spoke. For some reason, I began reminiscing about the younger me, the one who stood up to the seventh period bully in spite of knowing she would kick my "little white girl ass"; the me who sassed two muggers and offered her Bible instead of her purse despite their gun; the one who did a lot of things wrong but at least did something. She dominated at war ball and stood up for her principles regardless of what anyone thought.

"What happened to that girl?" I wondered aloud.

"I think of you as brave," my friend said, her saintliness warming our damp clothes and outshining the muck we both carried on our soles.

But bravery wasn't the issue. My lack of common sense often trumps a healthy sense of fear, something Mother said came from Daddy's side. But that is not the same thing as bravery. When I stood up to the seventh period bully, I wasn't afraid of losing or even concerned with winning. People would think what they would. I had to face myself every day, however. And though I had not sought out conflict nor dreamed of being labeled a rabble-rouser, it was not okay to stand by in the face of a wrong and do nothing.

Here's the thing: I thought by now—343 in dog years—I'd be past all that, beyond the reaches of what people thought of me, safely nested in a world that rotated on my own axis. I figured that as a woman of a certain age (WOCA)—which, according to Byron, is "neither old nor young," but according to Dickens "certainly aged"; however defined by Rubin as "fortyish and thereabouts thus able to initiate boys and young men into the beauties of sexual encounters" or the OED: "the age which it is not polite or necessary to further define"—my zip code would be in the Land of I Don't Give a Rat's Ass.

Although never expecting to go willingly into old age, the new address sounded seductive. Nirvana, baby! The ultimate season. The womanly state of being a certain age. No pesky constraints of youth, no trying to find yourself, no trying to find the right person to be yourself with, no breastfeeding battalions, no room mother relays, no PMS—neither perfect mother syndrome nor the other kind. There was even mention of epidermal transcendence, an understanding that surpassed crow's feet. How could I not bring my aging cup before such mixologists and raise a glass to this heavenly cocktail of enlightenment? The Wocatini and its inebriate promises of wisdom according to Oprah, self-knowledge according to Kim Cattrall, and comfort in worn-out, saggy skin, according to Susan Sarandon, rivaled anything that flowed out of that Old Augustinian Fountain.

How could I not charge headlong into such Elysian Fields? Especially when, according to Lauren Hutton, the sex is better because "you learn how to, you know, work the vehicle better."

But it is Toni Morrison's sirenic revelation that calls loudest to me: "At eighty-one, I don't feel guilty about anything."

Morrison is there, in the Land of I Don't Give a Rat's Ass, where I thought I'd be, but it is Tia, my sixteen-year-old deaf, blind, and incontinent Chihuahua, not me, who channels Morrison. Tia uses her three teeth as she pleases and does not bother herself with sanctioned pads of elimination or suggested slumber locations. She doesn't even let furniture alter her course. And if my husband and I happen to be sleeping when she hits a snag and needs assistance returning from a midnight meditation through the doggy door, that is our problem, not hers. Only in the last year has she become a canine Zen master, but she's able to stand so still that I sometimes wonder if she's died on her feet. She has such a peace in those moments that I wish she could tell me what she knows, a tiny black and white furry statue, unmoving but still standing as she stares at something I can't see.

⁓

"I'm just glad to be here," a friend from high school said as she sat across from me, her head more peach fuzz than feathers, though she'd called herself a duck. I'd fretted whether the gift—a pair of poinsettias, one for each ta-ta—was funny, but I shouldn't have worried. A woman who walks between two and seven miles every day while undergoing chemo isn't fazed the least by seasonal plants, however tasteless. This was a brave woman, one not afraid to bitch-slap cancer.

"I don't know how you did it. I take a daily stimulant and I couldn't walk that far. I can't imagine how bad chemo must be."

She leaned in and I felt myself pulled toward her like a human magnet. "Chemo isn't so bad," she said, lowering her voice. Then she whispered, "But menopause. That's some shit."

None of us know how much time we have left, but according to my online life expectancy results, I am a little more than halfway done. With the first part gone—divided away like the top shell of an oyster, it occurs to me that I am not the calloused insensitive woman I'd hoped to become. I am in fact growing more open than I care to admit—even more vulnerable than I desire. My reaching a certain age has made me, in a word, a woman on a half shell.

The "V" word is difficult for me to say—vulnerable. But I know the quiz won't work without it. Sacrifices are no substitute. Not even the trading of a university job and a house on a lake for a life next to goats in a 150-year-old insulation-less house. Or saying good-bye to one's first garden before the full harvest. It takes more than pain of loss and more than promise of second blooms to become vulnerable. It requires honesty.

My husband stares at me. We were complicit in the lie that it gets easier.

I'd grown up in grocery stores; he'd grown up in the fields. But I wanted the connection between reaping and sowing to be more than metaphorical, so he broke the ground loose until I could dig by hand. Until I said it was enough, he kept tilling beside me. A waste of time? Love in action? Good exercise? Something else?

It was time to answer the question. "You know I want both—body and brain."

He knows. He also knows that I hate limits and boxes and rules but desperately need them to push against. He raises an eyebrow.

And I know that, as superficial as it will sound, I have to be honest.

"Body," I finally say. "I think it's my weaker link."

One of the first things I did when we moved back to the city and bought our new home was build large squares in the backyard that I filled with bags of dirt. The summer harvest has come and gone, but it'll be a while yet before the freeze of winter sets in. However, some nights get pretty cold, so when Tia did not come in last night, I went outside to find her. She was in the far corner of the yard, back past my raised beds now filled mostly of compost and a few stubborn onions, standing in her statue-like pose. Instead of scooping her up, though, I joined her and stood stock-still beside her and stared into the dark. I can't say that I felt peace while standing there, but when I saw nothing, I did not flinch.

At eighty, Gloria Steinem says she wouldn't do anything differently, but she would do it faster.

Before we get to question number seven in the quiz, I announce to my husband, "I'm going to vandalize the sign this weekend." My husband smiles but does not offer to join. He just reads the next question.

Maybe I'm the only one who tells myself this lie: it gets easier. Maybe for some, it actually does. All I know is that midway through, this is what I see from my vantage point: two people in midlife on a couch, relationships no easier than they ever have been or will be, many questions still ahead, and them still pretending to be smarter and wiser and better, and of course more in love—when maybe what they really are is only older, their senses fine-tuned by age and the increasing need to keep going, even as they fumble their way into the dark.

The Walker

Ellen Morris Prewitt

The sand shakes beneath my feet. A ribbed shell startles my big toe, and I shift my foot, but my step fails to land in a safe place, and my arch retreats from an edge sharp as shrapnel. In front of me, my marching shadow appears the same as always...except even in the indistinct outline the jiggle of my wobbly thighs is visible.

Who cares?

I'm accomplishing something I learned to do at twelve months old but lost over the last few years: I'm walking barefoot on the beach.

My rheumatologist squinted at me and asked, "You weren't a linebacker for the New York Giants and I didn't know it, were you?"

I had developed a limp. A pain squirted up my groin when I walked. High heels were the problem, I concluded when it first began. At the time, I walked for a living. Well, it was a paltry living, but, aside from practicing law, it was the most lucrative gig I'd ever had. Specifically, I did runway work in Memphis, Tennessee. In this modeling job, which I came to late in life, the walk was everything. Your attitude, your attractiveness to the audience—it all depended on the walk. My walk depended on my wiggle. I'm not tall, so for my height, I relied on high heels.

Then the day came when good sense—and pain—told me I needed to give up modeling, at least for a while. Runway work wasn't particularly taxing; models are on and off the catwalk, lickety-split. Trunk shows, when you silently perambulate around a store for, oh, seven hundred hours, were another matter—the next day, I would be bent over in pain. Give it a rest, I figured, a chance to recover. Sensible me, I patted myself on the back, the part of my body I thought was causing the problem.

As the months passed, I had to quit rollerblading. The dog walks became shorter and shorter, until I could only make it to the end of the block. I would set out walking to the grocery store and turn back, old habits dying hard. Walking in groups, I lagged behind. Twisting, I entered the car butt-first, like an old person. High heels became a thing of the past, anything other than a flat shoe a negotiated event: was the pain worth it? One by one, I gave away the shoes my wardrobe once revolved around—standing naked in the closet, I would build my daily outfit from the feet up—until the only impractical shoes I owned were my Carlos Santana stiletto-heeled boots, sartorial evidence of my refusal to entirely abandon that phase of my life. At one point, I had asked my husband to engrave on my tombstone, "She could dance in high heels." Now my husband would have to add what I foresaw as a crudely carved addendum: "until she couldn't."

Time had quickly accordioned and I, younger than most, was experiencing the loss of mobility. Arthritis was eating my hips, though the trajectory presented not as injury but as aging. "You have the hips of a seventy-year-old," my doctor told me at age fifty-one. When I repeated this to a friend, she said, "My mother's seventy, and she walks just fine." Her observation didn't survive my dropping from a woman who adored yoga's challenging crow pose to cheating at gentle yoga classes to being unable to lever myself onto a mat. Thanks to my wonky pelvis, lifting weights brought pain. I watched, fascinated, as my muscled arms softened, puffing into loaves of bread. Sex was challenging; I moved from position to position with all the fluidity of a rolling block of ice. I couldn't pick up anything off the floor; if I dropped an artichoke in the produce department, there it lay until a kind stranger came along. Eventually, I became too unstable to walk barefoot on the beach, tennis shoes required.

Even so, I thought, how bad could it be? I had arthritis in my hips, that's all. "Plain ol' arthritis," I'd say when people searched for an explanation more exotic—and less likely to happen to them—such as rheumatoid arthritis or necrosis. Yet by age fifty-seven, six years after the football question, when I had run through every supposed remedy in the world ("Yes," I would say as people asked if I'd tried acupuncture, cinnamon, yoga, Pilates, physical therapy, fish oil, TENS electrical units, pectin and grape juice, physical therapy, cold packs, ginger, meditation, stretching my foot muscles, cortisone injections, chiropractors, physical therapy, forgoing vegetables of the nightshade family, shoe inserts, walnuts, deep tissue massage, ibuprofen, swimming, glucosamine, glucosamine-chondroitin, cayenne pepper topical cream, Rolfing, magnesium, and more I'm sure I've forgotten), I was scheduled for one hip surgery in January, the next in June.

I did not want to have this surgery. Right up to the moment, I kept hoping some sort of miracle would take it from me. Many assured me the routine surgery was no big deal—I would smile as friends chirped comfort, thinking, no one's gonna lay your ass on a table, insert metal into your body, force you into three months of rehab, then do it all over again. Others greeted my news with a story about the terrible experience a friend's cousin's wife had with her hip replacement that left her in a wheelchair (hint: don't say these things).

When I told the writing group I facilitate, the one in which all the writers have personally experienced homelessness, I received a different reaction. We were in the dining room of the support center where we meet; the writers were wrapped in coats and baggy sweaters to ward off the chill tinting the air. November was winding down, Christmas around the corner. As I explained why I would be absent for a while, one of the writers stared at me and then interrupted my spiel. "They're gonna cut on you?" he asked, incredulous.

Finally, I thought. Someone gets it. Writing group, as usual, keeping it real: what had happened to me was crap and was about to get worse.

✍

Here's what they do. (Warning: Stop reading now if you might have an upcoming hip surgery and would rather not carry the images of the specifics in your brain.)

First, they saw off the head of your femur. Next they ream the femur out. Then they take a hammer and—wham!—they hammer a metal spike into the femur. Somewhere in the process they also replace the ball and socket of the hip joint.

"Have you ever seen your x-rays?" my surgeon asked.

I'd been waiting in the exam room for my checkup following my second surgery. To kill time I was studying the chart of the human body on the back of the door, vaguely wondering if they'd given me an adult hip or a child's hip—I'm not a big person. When the surgeon appeared, I mustered up the courage to ask him to show me on the chart exactly what one replaced in a "hip replacement." That's when he inquired about the x-rays.

"Way back at the beginning," I told him, remembering how little I could discern from the misty x-rays of the eroded joint and protruding bone spurs.

The surgeon led me around the corner to a nook behind the nurses' station. He rolled up a chair and sat, opening my x-rays on his computer. I leaned over his shoulder, studying the screen. Sure enough, there was the metal rod and the ball. Something else too.

"That's a screw!" I exclaimed, seeing the tiny cap and threaded body of a screw clear as day.

156

"Yes," he replied, mildly offended. "That's why you could get out of bed and walk the first day."

I got so tickled. I'd been telling everyone, "Oh, my surgeon is the best. He teaches four techniques at the university, and he recommends this one because it gives the best results, allowing patients to walk again very quickly." Me, talking as if it were some amazing technological feat or dexterous slight of surgical hand.

It was a screw.

Everyone wants to know why. Why did a slim woman who didn't pound the pavement or do other repetitive activity (and wasn't, in fact, a New York Giants linebacker) wind up with crappy hips? My surgeon says my hips went to shit because my butt is so big. Okay. He actually said my pelvis is out of proportion to the rest of my torso. In other words, the wiggle that snagged me my modeling job, the wiggle that once led a man in the hallway of the Westin St. Frances Hotel to declare, "If you could can that wiggle and sell it, you'd be a millionaire," the same wiggle did me in. Karma, as they say.

I twist open the bottle of vitamin E gel caps. Aiming a small gold safety pin, I pierce the end of an amber orb and pinch. Liquid oozes into a small plastic disc filled with lotion. Using my pinky, I swirl the mixture then fill my palms, rubbing this concoction of my own making into the Frankenstein scars on my hips. I don't want to bore you with the indignities of the surgeries. One went well; one not so well. I'm eternally grateful for the inconsistency as it leaves me unable to judge or pontificate on how one "should" recover from a hip replacement. Everyone is different, and—similar to the impetus to rate some difficulties worthy of compassion and others not—blaming patients for their form of recovery doesn't seem very helpful. By hook or crook, I had emerged on the other side of the surgeries. As my grandson says, my wiggle had been fixed. But as I slick my skin with the healing lotion, I consider: how eager should I be to erase the evidence of my arthritic journey?

In my slow descent toward surgery, I spent a lot of time in medical clinics. I would wait at the elevator while an old woman bent over a walker or an old man leaning on a cane approached. She pushed the walker across the thin carpet; he drug his foot. The elevator arrived, and I held the door. I wasn't being patient—patience implies an overcoming of urgency. These were my people, those who traveled the earth at half-metered time. When they navigated ahead of me in the lobby, I dawdled so as not to run up on them—the sixth sense of us slower ones can detect irritation barreling down upon us. Making it to the precarious outdoors, I too lifted my foot to negotiate the curb, proud of my accomplishment. After a while I adopted the stare of the aged, studying passing joggers, wondering if they appreciated the gift of youthful motion.

Now, I'm on the upswing. Yes, the wind still slows my walking progress and toe drags spark alarm. I'm relearning not only how to traverse up the incline but, surprisingly, down as well. I sidestep slippery puddles and hesitate when I spy slick pine needles, but sometimes I venture into the grass, scanning for holes, the tiny muscles that protect one's balance still not quite ready to tackle unevenness. I can, however, ascend the stairs holding a coffee cup in my hand.

On off days when I'm not covering distance, I do the Farmer's Walk, which involves carrying a heavy object in your hand (think of a farmer and a sloshing pail of milk). Sometimes I get confused in my mind and think of it as the Fireman's Walk. My cousin's child is a fireman. He competed on a TV show where, basically, the contestants try to kill each other in acts of extreme athleticism and whoever comes out alive wins. When he and I were young, we'd roll in the grass on the front lawn, playing. He won the TV competition. I think about his feats of endurance as I wobble down the sidewalk with pride. It's subjective, what each of us can accomplish. The warm flush of happiness, I think, is the same regardless of how others might judge the difficulty.

This feeling of a second chance is strong enough to make me weep. In fact, it did make me weep. When a physical therapist in a long line of physical therapists asked me to list activities I'd lost, then asked me how it would feel to regain those activities, I burst into tears. I never expected to lose my mobility so suddenly—none of my family has arthritis; my mother still plays tennis in her eighties; my older sister hikes up mountains; my younger sister rides the James River rapids standing on a paddle board—nor, honestly, did I expect to regain it.

One bright fall afternoon, as I'm skimming down the sidewalk of our neighborhood practicing the figure eight pattern healthy hips should trace, I pass my first Memphis home where I lived fifteen years ago. Here, I shoved off on my rollerblades, took the stairs two at a time. Now when I stride forward with my new strength, it's as if I've broken a barrier into the past. I recall John Cheever's famous time-warping short story, "The Swimmer," trying to remember if he swam into the past or the future, or simply swam out of his life.

Call me The Walker. This is my new intention: walking long distances, for several hours, with specific destinations. For this purpose, I bought a gold nylon backpack with leather shoulder straps. On walking days, I fill the backpack with a water bottle and my driver's license, sometimes a protein bar. Zipping shut the outside pouch that holds my cell phone, I hoist the pack on my back. Now I'm ready to explore the long thin sidewalk along the Mississippi River or the hush of the Old Forest at Overton Park or the shaded Greenbelt once home to noisy train tracks. Although this walking has beneficial side effects, it's not exercise. It's more about setting a goal and walking towards it. But...sometimes mid-trek I see myself urgently walking, walking, and I wonder if I'm not actually running away.

Following my first surgery, I experienced a moment of panic as intense as I've ever felt. I had stalled, leaning over the walker, my nightgown swaying at my calves. I'd made it to the end of the bed, but to reach the bathroom I had to turn the corner. Pain riveted me in place, and my brain cried out, *What have you done to yourself?* There was no going back, no chance to shout, "Stop! I made a mistake. I can live with the slowness. Just don't make me do this." I didn't want to accept what had happened to me. I didn't want to get through this setback to a new, more vibrant me. I wanted to return to the person I'd been before the whole thing started, never having been here at all.

Perhaps this moment of terror was my glimpse of what Deborah Koehn Loyd in her book *Your Vocational Credo* (Inter-Varsity Press, 2015) calls the "wild unknown" of irreversible change, a crucial moment in my life trajectory that can usher in transformation. If so, my pell-mell striding toward health and safety is misguided.

Exhibit A: Sometimes, when I find myself in the vicinity of a woman approximately my age walking with shoulders hunched, upper body straining forward at a tilt, I feel it creeping up on me. Smugness. A deliberate decision to put a pep in my step. A desire to lengthen my stride. Showing off my new hips, letting my walking do the ugly talking: "I'm not old like you."

But I am. It's a game I cannot win. The metal hips will continue to pump like pistons, but my side will stitch. My heart with its slow, steady pulse will beat on, but my scoliotic back will curve with a dowager's hump, limiting my ability to scan for danger and once again forcing tiny steps. The slow slide into infirmity will spin around, and one day I will return to where I was—feeble, limited, believing I can, only to realize I can't. When that happens, I will become like my father-in-law, bragging about walking clear across the nursing home lobby.

Youth is ignorant. When we're in it, we look at those around us who struggle, and we tell ourselves it won't happen to me—if I eat right and exercise and do yoga and take vitamins and meditate, I'll stay strong and independent. I'll be the exception. I will not grow old. That's a lie, and now I know it.

᷈

The end of Ocean Isle Beach is washing away. By a quirk of nature, the beach doesn't parallel the mainland as most islands do. The island, which my family has visited every summer since I was in the eleventh grade, juts perpendicular into the Atlantic Ocean. Natural erosion—and unexpected storms—eat at the curved point. At the tip of the island, the beachfront road that was once First Street is now Third Street.

A yearly beach activity has always been a walk to the end of the island to survey the damage inflicted since the prior year. "The Death March," a non-fan called it. I've never measured the walk, never even timed it. This year for the first time in many years, I set off.

Soon, my legs relax into a rhythm. The tide is out, an essential ingredient to my plan, giving me a flat place to walk. My mind flits all over the place, taking in the eddies of tidal pools, the patches of seashells. Everyone in sight seems to be running. The redheaded toddler escaping his dad. The dog bounding off the leash. Seagulls with their toothpick legs pitty-pattying across the sand. As if being in the presence of the infinite ocean makes us want to fling our arms wide and bolt, no purpose except unfettered motion. I measure my progress by the yellow house, then the blue umbrella, now the man in the lounge chair, his legs splayed in the ocean's tide. The sea oats wave on the dunes, and memories of crab fishing as a child, bodysurfing an incoming wave, phosphorescent foam riding midnight surf float in and out of my brain.

When the island curves and ends, I gaze at the strait separating me from the adjacent island. With the tide in retreat, water has ebbed from the cul-de-sac. I think of what I've lost to the faulty hips: comfort from believing I wouldn't get a disease because it didn't run in my family; the illusion of control over my health; the "we" of belonging to a fit, athletic clan.

I ponder, too, what I've gained: the relief of knowing willpower can't cure everything; a reservoir of kindness towards the infirm; freedom from having to identify as fit and athletic; a glimpse of the final edge on which we all teeter.

Beachcombers gather seashells along the damp shoreline, collecting their booty. The next island silently waits, and I understand there is no escape. The gradual decline awaits us all. The only question is, as I move forward in my newly resurrected state, can I walk the path with grace, whether or not I wear high heels?

A Second Chance at Empty-Nesting

Susan Marquez

Once a woman gives birth, her life is no longer her own. That doesn't mean her dreams are no longer valid, or that her life as an individual no longer matters. The truth is that it matters more than ever, but often dreams are put on hold, while days are filled with meals, skinned knees, school meetings, soccer, ballet, first communion, first loves, and rebellion. The whole while, the object of the game is to raise responsible adults, send them out into the world to find their own way, then revel in a job well done while trying to figure out how to spend the rest of your life in a meaningful and fulfilling way.

On August 29, 2008, I was happy. I was at peace. I knew that everyone I cared about was all right. My husband, Larry, was content at his job. Both of my children seemed to be on a good path. My younger child, Joseph, was settled in at his second college (so far) and seemed to like his classes. My older child, Nicole, was blissfully happy in New York City and finally on the brink of supporting herself financially. She had moved there in January, with high hopes of performing on Broadway. It was slow going at first, and we subsidized her rent more often than not. But she was determined to make it on her own, earning her Pilates teaching certification and a job at a fitness center and, with that, the income she needed to be independent.

I was getting used to being an "empty-nester," and really enjoying it. It's as though I was finished with one thing and ready to start the next. I had been so busy raising children and having a career and running our home for the past twenty-five years that I had not taken the time to dream of what my own future may hold. What did I want to do with my life? How did I see life for Larry and me going forward? What were the things that most interested me? How could I incorporate those things into my life? Just thinking about it all energized me. I was excited about the life ahead of me.

One evening, Larry came home from work early and we enjoyed a rare night out. We went to hear a French-inspired jazz group perform at a coffee shop/bar not far from our home. While there, we ran into friends and I felt content that we lived in a place where people knew us. I loved the familiarity of being surrounded by people I recognized but didn't necessarily know. They were the same people I saw in the grocery store, the dry cleaners, and at events in our community. I also loved knowing that, in a crowded room, there were several people we did know—from our kids' school, dance classes, soccer, church, committees—people who knew us well enough to know our kids were out of the house and that we were enjoying a night out.

We even ran into friends of Nicole's. Friends who had transcended college days and remained friends now that they all had jobs. Her friend Danny asked how she was doing in New York. "She's too busy now to call me, I suppose." He sighed. That wouldn't do for me. I always stressed the importance of true friends to Nicole, and the importance of making the effort to reach out and stay in touch. I dialed Nicole's number, ready to hand the phone over to Danny when she answered. But she didn't. Instead, I got her voice mail.

When we returned home late that evening, I called again. No answer. I tried not to let my mind wander. I refused to let myself worry about her. "She's an adult, living her life. She'll tell me all about it in the morning." I prayed the prayer I prayed each night since Nicole spent a semester abroad in France. "Lord, wherever she is, whatever she is doing, please take care of her."

The morning came, and Larry went to work while I busied myself cleaning the house. It was a sunny Saturday, and I made reservations to eat at a new restaurant that evening to celebrate Larry's birthday the week before. Two nights out in a row! All day I had a wonderful feeling that my life was finally my own. My job raising my children was done. They were pursuing their dreams and now it was time for me to follow mine.

When the phone rang about 1:30 p.m., those thoughts ceased. My world came to a complete stop. All the dreams of an exciting life ahead were pulled out from under me. Just getting through the next moment seemed impossible. I went from happy to hell in thirty seconds flat.

What was I supposed to do? Who was I supposed to call? I was not prepared for this. Who really is? There is no instruction manual for what to do when you find out your daughter has fallen from the roof of her apartment building, that she was alive the last time the detective spoke with someone in the emergency room, but that's all he could tell me.

The next few hours were a blur. Call the emergency room at Harlem Hospital. *What do you mean you don't have a Nicole Marquez?* Is this a sick joke? Call Larry at work. Call the emergency room again. Maybe I should call her roommates. *I don't know their telephone numbers, let alone their last names. I had asked Nicole numerous times to give me that information, just in case.* Talk to a doctor who asks if she has any distinguishing marks. Do a mental body scan to try to recall birthmarks. Stop on her wrist, where a tattoo of a star the size of a quarter is permanently inked. The tattoo that made me so mad and sad when I discovered its presence. Tell the doctor about the tattoo. Which wrist, he asks. Is he serious? *I don't know.* I had tried to forget the damn thing was there.

As I waited for Larry to come home, I stood in Nicole's room, trying to remember when all was right with the world. A picture frame on her dresser caught my eye. It was a picture of me, holding Nicole as a newborn. I was the age she was that day, twenty-five. I hadn't been around many newborns in my life, so having one of my own was a bit overwhelming. The day we were released from the hospital after she was born, Nicole's godmother, Carol, was with me. She still laughs at the look of panic on my face. "I can't go home yet," I whined to the nurse. "I have no idea how to take care of her. I don't even know what to feed her!"

Larry and I didn't put her in a car seat on the way home. We didn't own one. That wasn't a requirement in 1983. I sat in the back seat, holding my little bundle, and I knew in that moment my world would never be the same. At home, we marveled at how tiny she was, and how beautiful. To know that she was totally dependent on us for everything was intimidating, but at the same time, it helped to create a bond so strong that I felt it deep within my heart. *I'll always be here for you, little one.*

It's a rare thing when space and time are obliterated, when the world as we knew it turns upside down and inside out and nothing is or will ever be the same again. Time stands still. Don't think about the future; you might not like what you see. Don't focus too much on the past, because it no longer exists. Be here, now. But where is here? This place where love and hope and complacency are being sucked out of my soul. It's a surreal time when a tragedy occurs, when the loss of what was and what used to be floods our being and there is absolutely nothing we can do. I try, but I can't even pray.

My arrival in New York was thirty-two hours after the first phone call from the detective. It was 8:30 p.m., and Larry, who had flown out five hours after me (I got the last seat on the early flight), had been in New York for a few hours already. My trip had not been so easy. A long layover in Baltimore. Confusion with the car service at the airport. An idiot driver who drove around the city with no idea where the hospital was but thought it would be a good idea for us to pull over and pray together. Larry and I finally met in the lobby of New York Presbyterian Hospital. Nicole had been transferred there from Harlem Hospital, the level one trauma center closest to her apartment. She was upstairs in the Neuro ICU, where nurses were inserting a port in her chest for intravenous medications.

A flurry of activity continued for the next few hours. At 4:00 a.m. we were introduced to a young neurosurgeon in the hallway. Dr. Angevine looked like he was about nineteen years old. He was very serious and spoke confidently about the procedure to stabilize Nicole's neck, including the possibility that her voice may never sound the same again, and her neck would most likely not have much mobility. As we signed the release forms, Dr. Angevine asked if we had any questions. All Larry could muster was "Are you any good?" The doctor allowed a half smile across his lips. "Yeah, I'm pretty good."

Nicole was scheduled for surgery at 6:00 a.m. By the time Dr. Angevine left to go rest for a while, the Neuro ICU had quieted down a bit. Lights had been dimmed and the only noise was that of the ventilator and heart monitor. Soft beeps in the darkened room meant our daughter's heart was still beating.

Despite falling six stories, Nicole looked amazingly beautiful. Her face was unscathed, and I noticed that her eyebrows had been waxed recently. She was still wearing mascara from the audition she had been to before she got home and realized she didn't have her keys. We learned later that she had tried calling her roommate, but got no answer, so she decided to go to the roof, a place where she and her roommates sunbathed and studied their lines. Somehow, she fell off the roof of the building. The *how* didn't matter. Knowing what happened wouldn't change the outcome. Nicole lay in the filthy airshaft of the building for eight hours before the building's superintendent discovered her Saturday morning. Several vertebrae in Nicole's neck were crushed, as was a vertebrae in her lower back. Her pelvis was broken, and she had broken several ribs on the left side. One of the ribs punctured her lung, which collapsed. It turns out that was her most life-threatening injury. For now, all I could see from the fall was some bruising and scratches along her left arm. She had dirt between her fingers and under her fingernails.

I asked for washcloths to clean her. The nurses gave me warmed disposable cloths that I used to wash her face, arms, and hands. I took my time, rubbing the warm cloths across her beautiful olive skin. I recalled the first time I gave her a bath when she was a baby. I had gently undressed her and placed her on a towel on our bed, where I cleaned each arm and leg, wiping her gently and marveling at how beautiful her baby skin was. It was dark olive, which she got from Larry. She also had pink cheeks and dark eyes that looked like polished coal. Here we were, twenty-five years later, and I was bathing her once again. She was once again dependent on others for everything. Her skin was still beautiful, and as I bathed her, her eyes fluttered open. Long lashes framed coal black eyes that looked at me trustingly, lovingly. Nicole knew she was in the hospital, and she knew I was there, caressing her and soothing her. *Some things never change.*

Over the next few months we gradually adapted to our new normal as we went from an intensive care unit to a step-down hospital in Jackson, Mississippi, and finally on to the Mississippi Methodist Rehabilitation Center. In the beginning, no one could predict the outcome. The original goal was simply to keep Nicole alive. Next was to stabilize her neck, then her lower back, requiring surgeries to prevent further injury. It took time for her to recover from her injuries and from the surgeries so that she could begin to heal. The next goal was rehabilitation. We all mentally prepared for the worst—life in a wheelchair. We prayed for the best—complete mobility. The prayers worked, because on January 21, 2009, Nicole walked out of rehab.

Probably the hardest transition was coming home. Nicole went away to college when she was nineteen and only visited home when she had to. It's not that she hated home, but she was so excited about exploring the world. She had six years of freedom, starting with her college days and the semester she spent studying abroad in France, then on to acting apprenticeships at the Berkshire Summer Theatre Festival in Stockbridge, Massachusetts, and The Actors Theatre in Louisville, Kentucky. She moved home for a few months and worked to save money to relocate to New York. She announced in December 2007 that she'd be moving in January. She had everything arranged—her plane ticket and an apartment with roommates from her time at the theatre in Louisville.

Being home again, in the room where she spent her teenage years, was difficult for Nicole. Having her there, and having the responsibility of tending to her every need, was difficult for me as well. It was like having a newborn all over again, but this one weighed 100 pounds and could talk. I still had to bathe her, brush her teeth, fix her hair, and help her get dressed. Her spinal cord injuries temporarily affected all of her bodily functions, which meant I also had to change diapers once again. And just as when she was a newborn, I was often overcome with strong emotions, amazed at the miracle of life. It was a miracle to me that she was born twenty-five years earlier. It was certainly a miracle that she was alive now.

Just as when she was a newborn, I had to hurry to bathe and dress myself each morning, plan my day around her schedule, nap when I got a chance, and be prepared to drop what I was doing to tend to her needs. At first I couldn't leave her at home alone, so I was limited on where I could go and when. I depended on Larry to pick up groceries on his way home. My life and my time were not my own. I struggled to be positive. My mind tried to wander to some dark places. On the one hand, I was angry at Nicole for pulling such a stupid stunt. What the hell was she thinking? Who goes to the roof of a building late at night to try to go down a fire escape? On the other hand, I was deeply grateful that she had not only survived but was doing so well.

I had been warned that traumatic events such as this can have a devastating effect on a marriage. Larry and I had been married for twenty-eight years and one week at the time of Nicole's accident. To this day, Larry is the nicest person I've ever known. We met in college and married the next year. He left his family in Venezuela to make a life with me in Mississippi. He has strong family values and loves his children with every fiber of his being. Nicole's accident was hard on Larry, especially since he was privy to the difficult details concerning her condition in the hospital. He purposely shielded me from learning how critical her condition was because he wanted me to be as positive and upbeat as possible for Nicole. We clung to each other for support, and our love for each other grew even stronger. I don't know how I would have managed without him.

As she grew stronger, Nicole needed me less and less. She felt a strong need to be independent again. Her struggle wasn't always easy, but it wasn't easy for me either. Although my life had been disrupted in the most unsettling way when she fell, I had also been given a gift of sorts. When Nicole moved to New York, I accepted that we might see her once or twice a year. It was our hope that we'd visit Nicole in New York and celebrate her performances on Broadway. Or perhaps she'd fly home for Christmas each year. But after spending all day, every day with her for a couple of years after her accident, helping her with almost everything she did, being by her side every step of the way, cheering her on as she regained more independence, I had a hard time letting go. I brought her into this world and then set her free to follow her dreams in New York. I essentially watched her rebirth as she came out of the darkness of a terrible accident that left her critically ill with traumatic injuries. I supported and encouraged her as she fought to regain the use of her body, secretly aching inside, mourning the girl who used to run, skip, jump, climb, swing, twirl, and *dance*. It hurt to watch her painstakingly squeeze a strip of toothpaste onto her toothbrush. It hurt to watch her struggle to put on a shirt or a pair of pants. It hurt to have to help her with a zipper or buttons. It hurt to have to help her go to the bathroom because she couldn't do it by herself. It hurt. Every day. I ran out of patience often. I would fix her hair, only to have her disapprove of the job I did. So I would fix her hair again, even though I thought it looked fine the first time. I lost patience when I'd help her get dressed and then she'd want to change clothes. I lost patience when we were headed out the door, and she'd have to go back and use the bathroom. I had to remind myself over and over again that I could be putting flowers on her grave instead of tying her shoes for the fourth time today.

Nicole has moved on now. She has found love with a patient man who is amazed by her story and her determination. She has become a successful motivational speaker and travels the country sharing her message of perseverance and hope. And as she has become more independent, she has put more space between us, which makes me sad.

I can't help worrying about her because, when I didn't, she fell six stories off the roof of her apartment building. But I am learning to let go. While Nicole was recovering and going through rehabilitation, our son found his way as well. He changed colleges a couple of times before landing at Millsaps College in Jackson where he flourished. He graduated in May 2015 and moved to Arizona for a corporate job that he loves. My husband and I had an empty nest once again. And once again, I found myself in a position of defining my dreams.

While I didn't fall off the building, I did go through a trauma. I had to live through the fear, learn to let go and handle what happens on any given day. I am certainly stronger now. I have learned many lessons that I feel make me a better person. I know I can walk through hell and survive. I know I can be angry with God and he won't turn his back on me. I know I can be frustrated with Nicole and still love her with all my heart. I live in the present more than I ever have, and I'm actually more comfortable doing that. I don't dwell on the "*what ifs*" in life. It doesn't matter. All I have is the "*what is.*" In my life, it is the fact that I'm relatively healthy. I have a husband who loves me. My children are okay. I'm free to follow my dreams.

Through posting on Caring Bridge, a personal health journal that rallies friends and family through any kind of health issues, I rediscovered my love of writing. Although I had been a professional freelance writer since 2001, writing about Nicole's journey each day was a soul-soothing exercise in hope and faith. I felt connected to the journal's readers through their guestbook entries. After eighteen months of chronicling Nicole's amazing recovery and rehabilitation every day, I stopped posting on Caring Bridge and began a blog. I still marvel at Nicole's accomplishments in my writing, but I also post about subjects that are interesting to me in my own life journey. I am working on a book-length memoir about Nicole's ordeal from my viewpoint, sharing lessons I've learned. To help me with that, I've attended numerous workshops and seminars on creative nonfiction, book publishing, and marketing. Along the way I've met other writers who have become my "writing tribe," folks who understand the process and who support me and the others in our tribe in a way that makes my heart soar. I have grown more confident in my skills as a writer and have found opportunities to help others, including editing eight books and doing publicity for other authors. I am still doing freelance writing for magazines, newspapers, business journals, and trade publications.

I spend time with Nicole, occasionally assisting her on trips to do speaking engagements. She has become a sought-after motivational speaker, and I have helped her develop that career using my skills as a marketer and public relations professional. It is a wonderful feeling for me to see her on a stage in front of a live audience, sharing her story of perseverance and hope nationwide. She lives independently and has a fulfilling and happy life.

So let's try this again. I am happy. I am at peace. I know that everyone I care about is all right. My nest is empty, and my life is full!

To read more about Nicole's accident, visit www.caringbridge.org/visit/nicolemarquez as well as her website at www.nicole-marquez.com. Susan's blogs can be found at www.susanmarquez.blogspot.com and www.thewordblender.blogspot.com.

The Triskele

Sally Palmer Thomason

Three summers ago I purchased a small amulet of a triskele in a tiny gift shop in Rochefort en Terre, a beautifully restored medieval village atop a rocky hill in Brittany, the region in the northwest corner of France with deep Celtic roots. Even today, I rarely am without this small square-shaped charm, mounted on three leather thongs, clasped around my right wrist. Scratching through the remnants of human history from various lands, we find numerous intriguing symbols—the script in which the beliefs of a people were writ. Throughout the evolution of humankind, inspired souls have created visual images to capture their knowledge and beliefs. If a symbol was inherited or uncovered by a later culture, sensitive souls of that era stepped in to claim it as their own, often with a different connotation from that of an earlier time. Meister Eckhart, a revered philosopher-mystic who lived during the cusp between the thirteenth and fourteenth centuries, believed that when the soul wants to experience something, she throws out an image in front of her and then steps into it. The ancient symbol of the triskele's three interlocking spirals dates back to Neolithic times, eight to ten thousand years ago.

These three inseparable spirals, entwined in the center to make a whole, are like a whirligig in the wind, indicating continual motion. What intrigues me about the triskele is that it has been a significant symbol with multiple meanings for thousands of years. The ancient Celts believed the three spirals symbolized the cyclical progression of female life, Maiden-Mother-Crone. For Christians in the Dark and Middle Ages, the triskele symbolized Father-Son-Holy Ghost. Other traditions claim that the three spirals symbolize Earth-Water-Sky, Body-Mind-Spirit, Past-Present-Future, Life-Death-Rebirth, Mother-Father-Child, Power-Intellect-Love, or Creation-Preservation-Destruction. In every instance the three spirals, symbolizing a beginning, a middle fruition, and an ending, emanate from a central core in holistic completeness.

I find it extraordinary that today, a ten-thousand-year-old marking symbolizes what twenty-first century neuroscientists, psychologists, and philosophers are proposing. Dr. Clare Graves's research is foundational in the formation and understanding of spiral dynamics, an increasingly influential theory that the psychological development of the mature human being is an unfolding, oscillating, spiraling process, marked by progressive subordination of older, lower-order behavior systems to newer, higher-order systems as a human's existential problems change. In his latest book, *One Mind: How Our Individual Mind Is Part of a Greater Consciousness and Why It Matters,* Dr. Larry Dossey, a physician deeply rooted in the scientific world and a leading proponent of the role of consciousness and spirituality in health care, presents evidence that the dynamic spiral continues well beyond the development of the individual. The holistic completeness of the life of an individual entity is part of the larger holistic, ongoing life of the greater universe—spiral dynamics indicate not only the development of the individual but also the evolutionary development of humankind.

Contemporary physicists are showing how quantum entanglement connects us in mysterious, non-material, unquantifiable ways to all life from the very beginning of time. Each new beginning holds the seeds of past cycles in an ever-evolving holistic way, where the whole is greater than the sum of its parts. Energy is never lost; it just converts into different forms. As human beings we long to know who we are, not just in human terms but also in larger terms that connect us to the greater whole—an immanent God, expanding energy, love, wisdom, and truth, the divine consciousness that is within and without every mortal being. The eminent physicist David Bohm said, "Deep down the consciousness of mankind is one." For me the triskele's three spirals representing the beginning, the middle, and the end symbolize one iteration within the larger, ongoing cycle of ever-evolving life in this unfathomable universe.

Why three? Although in today's modern and post-modern world numbers are used only to indicate quantity, believers in sacred geometry, both ancient and contemporary, hold that numbers are more than a means to register quantity; each point within a number is significant in relation to the other parts within the whole of that number. Individual numbers provide insights into the mysteries of the unknowable forces that lie beyond common, observable knowledge and reveal certain designs and proportions that are woven into the fabric of nature in an undeniable, holistic relationship. They are symbols of the structure of the world and give insight into the affairs of humankind. Honoring the mystical power of three, Aristotle wrote, "The triad is…the very first which admits of end, middle and beginning, which are the cause of all completion and perfection being attained."

⁓

So what does all this have to do with second blooming?

In my late thirties, I read something written by Roberson Davies. I don't remember the exact wording or even the source, but it said something like this: as an individual approaches the age of forty, she or he smashes into a brick wall and falls to its base. Some folks have the courage and gumption to struggle up and climb over the wall. Others lie groveling, whimpering in the dirt at its base for the rest of their lives. When I read these words I had not heard the term "midlife crisis," coined by Carl Jung, the Swiss psychiatrist with a giant intellect and spirit, who observed that well-adjusted humans spend the first half of life developing a healthy ego and learning to adapt to cultural expectations in pursuit of social acceptance, pleasure, and material achievement. However, as individuals approached their fortieth year, they began to confront their own mortality and start to question the meaning and deeper purpose of their lives. (Astrologers note that Uranus, whose archetypal energies represent revolution and precipitous change, reaches its influential midpoint at forty-two years in its eighty-four-year cycle in a person's birth chart.)

I was a poster child for Jung's theory. It took me several years, some counseling, and some missteps before I muddled through my crisis and sailed forth into the "new me"—my second blooming, which lasted for some very happy years. And then, BAM, I hit another wall. Gabriel Garcia Marquez's wisdom confirms Dr. Graves's research on the spiral dynamics of human development. "Human beings," he writes, "are not born once and for all, the day their mother gave birth to them…life obliges them over and over again to give birth to themselves."

Now in my eighth decade, I have gone through not just one but several dramatic shifts in my circumstances, in my primary focus, and in my fundamental understanding and approach to life. A period of confusion, restlessness, and emotional/ physical/spiritual challenge preceded each shift. In time, I fortunately realized that these were periods of transition, natural phases in the cycles of living. Rather than visualizing my life on a line of time with the number of years I've lived marching straight along into the future, I realized that my life has been a complex of ongoing circles—some big, some small. My feelings, aspirations, even my health have followed a cyclical path, like the rings of a mature tree trunk, marking its life through the circular pattern of many seasons—good and bad. I've had wonderful periods of delightful and challenging adventure, affirming emotions, and personal accomplishments; followed by or intermingled with periods of self-doubt, dismal confusion, hurtful estrangements, and discouraging depression.

Multi-millenniums ago, human minds and hearts longing to find order in the midst of the chaos of their lives found the sun's annual cyclical pattern (as seen from earth) a reliable guide for planning their agricultural activities. Gradually, through observation and intuition, their astrologers, scholars, and mathematicians began to look to the planets, circling through the sky, to make sense of the impulses and longing in the lives of individuals. Carl Jung, impressed with the methodology and intuition of these astrologers, concluded that astrology was the psychiatry of the ancients.

Twenty years ago I had my astrological chart read by Alice Howell, a Jungian astrologist, well versed in ancient history and mythology. With effervescent enthusiasm she explored what the stars had to tell me about my character and life situation, spending a great deal of time on the importance of Saturn in my chart. Then in my mid-sixties, enjoying the fruits of my second blooming, I did not readily embrace her cheerful declarations about Saturnian impositions of limitations, structures, and boundaries on my life. Yet, after a great deal of reflection, I gradually came to a new understanding of what I initially interpreted as a negative encumbrance. I saw the value and necessity of limitations, realizing that one of the most extraordinary experiences of my life occurred when scuba diving in the Caribbean several years before. After donning flippers, tank, life vest, weights, and mask, I jumped off a dive boat, gradually descended to a depth of ninety feet, and hovered weightlessly over the tongue of the ocean, the 3,600-foot deep trench just off the island of Andros. It was a surreal float in infinity of suspended bliss. There was nothing but deepening blue below and an unending expanse of water and blue sky above. No demarcations of beginnings or endings, only a delightful column of bubbles rising in a stream of muted sunlight. My brush with eternity could only have been achieved through the lessons from Saturn—strict adherence to the rules for diving deep, wearing the necessary equipment, and paying close attention to the limitation of time that the oxygen in my tank allowed me to stay submerged.

Last year I again hit one of those walls of debilitating confusion and began to ask what now? At age eighty, my body had changed. I was losing flexibility and strength. My husband of sixty years, though sound of mind with a hearty spirit, had health issues and balance problems. I was losing close friends to Alzheimer's and death. For some reason, I was drawn to a further investigation of the symbolism of Saturn and was surprised when it led me to a deeper apprehension of the symbol of my triskele. Saturn in most western mythology is represented by Father Time carrying a sickle. Saturn's cycle around the sun from a geocentric perspective lasts a little over twenty-nine years. In an effort to visualize the potential symbolism of Saturn, I mapped its twenty-nine-year cycles over a timeline I'd drawn on a long sheet of paper where I had noted my development and activities through the years. The coherence of the cycles to my personal history was amazing. The cycles of Saturn as mapped on my timeline represented a triskele of my life—a symbolic image of my personal focus, activities, and growth during each twenty-nine-year period. Within the sacred view of numbers, three is the ability to observe our selves in relation to our own patterns and make decisions about how we want to shift those patterns. The realm of three becomes the place where awareness and perspective lead to growth and change.

1. *Beginnings*, birth to age twenty-nine: physical growth, growing awareness of self in comparison to others, preoccupation with looks and adornments, preoccupation with fitting in to my group, developing my intellect, honing new skills; fulfilling my cultural role—sexual awakening, marriage, birthing babies.
2. *Fruition*, age thirty to fifty-nine: nurture and care for my family, cultivation of friends, establishing a nice home, being a creative hostess, tennis, running, sailing, hiking, service in the community and church, shifting gears, developing a career, expanding my horizons, growth of the mind.
3. *Endings*, age sixty to eighty-nine: increased personal freedom, expanded travel, heightened intellectual and spiritual quests, recognition of God's spirit in every living thing, increasing physical limitations.

∽

One morning in the early part of my middle years, I noticed that a holly bush in our yard covered with an unusual profusion of brilliant red berries had lost most of its leaves. Cutting a branch to take to the nearest nursery, I learned that my holly, critically undernourished, sensed it was nearing its end. In an effort to perpetuate its species, the holly was creating as many seeds as possible. I do not equate my richly nourished life to that of my holly bush, but I am in an ending cycle, even though I may see the beginning of one more return of Saturn as my mother lived into her ninety-eighth year. However many years remain, I pray for wisdom in the throwing of my seeds for those who will follow in this ever-evolving holistic, oft hostile, puzzling, gratifying, extraordinary cycle of existence.

Dharma Slut

Jen Bradner

Forty years ago, in 1975, I was given the honorific title of "bastard" by the family courts in South Carolina. Allegedly, it was the last case of its kind in the original rebel state. My mother was a passionate soul who rarely passed up an opportunity for a radical romance. After months of marriage counseling with her minister, she fell in love with him, and so if it is true that a soul chooses its parents, this was the pair who intrigued me most. As a superstitious and quite religiously bent young woman, my mother believed that as a punishment for her spiritual crime against God, she had increased the probability that the offspring of Lucifer would come through her womb. When I was a newborn she checked me over for symbols and marks, and while she always held me near to her and loved me as I loved my Holly Hobby (after all, I was the souvenir left by the love of her life), she knew from the time I was three that she could not control me. Often my strong will challenged her in such a way that would frustrate her into violence. I, in essence, would act as my mother's karma and create a sort of hellish state for her in light of her manifestation.

In some traditions of lore, it is believed that humans enter into a lifetime with a predetermined quest that each soul designs for itself while still in the spirit state. In one respect, the Dharma, or the teachings, is the path that helps us find our way back to truth. It is the field guide of self-discovery that ignites the process we can use to remove or work through past pains and blockages that keep us from happiness. When we choose the path of self-discovery, we gain access to the introspection we need to live out each lifetime to our fullest potential.

It was revealed to me in spring 2011 during an astrological consultation in Sheep's Head, Ireland, that despite my tribal nature, in this life I orphaned myself. It would seem that my karma led me down the path of separation from my family, and so it's no wonder I was born into one that could not wait to see me spread my wings and fly away as the eagerness buried in my bones urged me to make my escape. The counter-side of this "path" naturally meant that there would always be a longing for family and the impulse to seek opportunities to join other families. Often through physical love I imagined a sense of kindredness. I found myself merging with identities constructed through relationships early on, first with girlfriends and eventually through sexual relationships with boys and then men. Each time a relationship ended, I would feel alone in the world all over again. At fifteen, the overwhelmingness of abandonment led me to rage and violence against another and against myself. Ashamed and unaware of the root of my darkness, I tried to take my life. This attempt led me to a doctor who spoke the magic words that would serve as my soul mantra on its journey back to its natural state—"You can never make someone love you. No amount of violence or force can make a person stay. If you want love, you must first learn to love yourself."

You must first learn to love yourself. A sound frequency my deafened ears could not hear, my pained spirit could not receive.

If I were to compare myself to a fairy-tale character, it would be Alice, often falling down the rabbit hole of another's plot and setting. I have opened up to a heart-centered frame of mind, which means attracting all sorts of people who need someone to walk alongside or to be pointed in the right direction. Too often, however, I find myself so enmeshed in the relationship that I struggle with the level at which I allow myself to give. Like a chakra mule, I work in realms of the other's karma until exhausted, depleted of resources and spiritual stamina and having gone too far to help realize another person's dream. As I discover this quality in myself, I choose to shut the door of my dharmic promiscuity and stay on my own trail. I vow to stand in my highest truth, and if the path I'm on or the hole I've fallen into isn't the path to my highest potential, affirmed by the light and peace it brings to me and those I love, I will kindly and with grace walk away.

Sifting through patterns of the past, determined to be who I am becoming in the world, I have finally reached the time to clear myself of the karmic residue and spiritual kleshas (negative habitual imprints). I am determined to be whole and vow to live in courage. I am a woman. My grey streak distinguishes me; at least that's what the lovely young man said while brushing color across my face, teaching me tricks to accentuate my beauty as my skin changes and my lines become more defined. I'm taking deeper breaths and forgiving deeper wounds.

Life continuously dishes a series of clues and lessons, and if we are dedicated to our growth and potential, it becomes an exciting quest of discovery. In nature I'm always amazed to find that often near a poisonous plant grows its sister plant that acts as a remedy. Like a solution embedded inside the riddle itself, when I am looking for the answer to a problem I am trying to understand, I generally start close to the source. For instance, if I feel that someone is dishonoring or dismissing me, I try to find instances in the present where I may be dishonoring or dismissing someone else. When I lose money, I give money away; if I need love, I give more away.

The past three years, which I will now refer to as the "lost years," have brought significant change to my life, possibly the lion's share of change I will come to know in my collective adulthood experience. It all started with a fantastical trip to Ireland in

September 2012 to tour a workshop I had designed titled "Energy of Money: Money Rehab." It was the most ethereal experience I had ever known, full of interactions and realizations about who and how I wanted to be presented to the world. During my visit I consulted with a Tarot reader who laid the three of hearts on the table, looked deeply into my eyes, and said, "Your mother. What's wrong with her?"

"She's okay, she's been sick but she's okay," I replied.

"Three weeks, you have three weeks to see her, I do not give dates and lottery numbers, I will give you three weeks."

I returned home from my trip and immediately reserved a cabin in the Smoky Mountains, the halfway point between my family and me. My mother, sister, brother, my son, and I spent four days in October watching black bears and cooking a Thanksgiving feast. We worked, fought, and cried our way through a family healing. A short while after, my mother passed away. These were in fact the "lost years." Kind of a blur. I completed a college degree, published a book, opened and closed a business, had a near-death experience, sent my daughter off to college, changed careers, became a CEO, discovered my "soul work," and entered the most dedicated love affair I've known. And those are just the headlines of my conscious mind. In this moment, now, that chapter of my life has ended. Today I am woman anew.

If what they say is true, that in the spirit state we choose our life's lessons and that we will never give ourselves more than we can handle, then I say with a pure heart that forty is a strong number, and I honor all the turns and passageways that led me here to this day. May the lessons reveal their love. May the path reveal our highest self. May we know peace.

V

Blooming in Careers and Community

I have heard it said that there are two times in your life when you stand a chance, in the face of whatever social forces struggle to get you in their grip, of becoming someone new, of creating your own personal universe through the sheer power of imagination and persistence: one is adolescence and the other is middle age. Maybe this is hogwash. Maybe it's profound truth. I certainly make no claim to know. What I do know is that very near my forty-third birthday, it dawned on me to look at the diaries I began when I was young.

—Margaret Sartor, *Miss American Pie* (p. 7)

Something Has to Die

Cassandra King

The time will come
When, with elation,
You will greet yourself arriving
At your own door, in your own mirror,
And each will smile at the other's welcome,
And say, sit here, Eat.
You will love again the stranger who was your self.
 —from "Love After Love," by Derek Walcott

In Greek mythology, Cassandra was a princess of Troy, considered the most beautiful of King Priam's daughters. Apollo was so taken with her that he bestowed on her the gift of prophecy. Even though Apollo was a great and mighty god, his gift came with a catch, as most gifts from his gender do. To receive it, Cassandra had to give herself to him. According to legend, she took his gift of prophecy eagerly, then refused to give Apollo what he'd asked for in return.

At this point in the story, I can't decide if Cassandra was a heartless flirt or just dumb as a post. Gods don't like being toyed with. Instead of rescinding his gift, Apollo turned it into a curse. Cassandra could foretell the future until the cows came in, but no one would believe her. In the end, her gift brought her nothing but misery, and she was shunned as a ranting, babbling idiot with no credibility whatsoever.

For a long time, I've been about as enamored with Cassandra as Apollo had been. It started the same time I fell in love with theater, when I was in charge of costumes for a college production of *Antigone*. Sophocles has an overabundance of fabulous characters in that play, but my favorite was Cassandra. Her tragic demeanor and dire fate struck a chord deep within my overly romantic soul, so naturally I gave her the best costumes—even better than Helen of Troy's, whose face had launched a thousand ships. Several years later, Cassandra reappeared when I took a graduate course in mythical archetypes and modern literature (or something along those lines). Again, I connected with Cassandra's story in a way that I couldn't even begin to explain. Our names, of course, are derivatives of the same Greek word (although no Greek ancestors have ever shown up in my family history). But it was more than that. There was just something about her that was *me*.

I was a returning adult in graduate school, in my early forties, a time that used to be considered midlife. I had written a collection of short stories for my thesis that I would one day turn into my first novel. I was teaching again after taking several years off to raise my kids and play the role of the good little preacher's wife. However, unknown to me at the time, my life was heading for some major changes. If Cassandra had appeared to me to foretell what was coming my way, I would not have believed her, the crazy old fool. I would have laughed in her face.

On the surface, midlife was a good time for me. Once I finished graduate school, I got a job I loved, teaching composition and working in the writing center of the beautiful little college I'd attended, and I was moonlighting as a reporter for a city newspaper. I had finished a novel and gone to New York (my first trip there!) to meet with an agent, who agreed to represent me. On the surface, all was well on the home front, too. My husband, the preacher-man, was doing well at a thriving, prosperous church in Birmingham, and I was trying not to let my writing/teaching interfere with my duties as the good little preacher's wife. The kids were good, or at least as good as preacher's kids can ever be. Our oldest son had gotten into the medical school of his choice and the youngest into the high school of his, while the middle son, age nineteen and in his first year of college, presented us with our first grandchild. My vibrant, seemingly healthy mother had died shortly after turning seventy. On the surface, at least, I was experiencing the typical, predictable events of that stage in life: some unbearably sad, others joy-filled, most mundane.

Beneath the surface was a different story. At that particular time in my life, I was a seething cauldron of misery and depression, compounded by guilt and self-hatred. If everything was going so well, then why was I so miserable? What a pathetic, whiny ingrate I'd turned out to be! During what should have been one of the best times of my life, I was functioning mostly on automatic pilot, so severely depressed it took all I could do to get out of bed and face each day. My health suffered as well; I was plagued with stomach ulcers and IBS, hospitalized for heart arrhythmias that left me shaken and scared. Although I don't know what I was scared of. If the heart problem had taken me out, I wouldn't have spent so much time trying to figure out the best way to do it myself. One of our churches, which was next door to the parsonage as most of them had been, had what I considered an ideal setup. I discovered an unused classroom with a fairly large gas heater for the size of the room. I figured it wouldn't take long in there. Of course I'd take some material with me so it would look as if I'd sought out a private space to work on my Sunday school lesson, and then the heater had malfunctioned. The poor preacher's wife, God rest her soul, doing the Lord's work when the Lord took her home. No one to blame, just a tragic accident.

The biggest strain for me during this time was not the health issues and the suicidal depression; it was the thing that had plagued me most of my adult life. What would people *think* if they knew how crazy I was? Fighting the depression was nothing compared to the effort it took to put up a good front. I had been doing so for many, many years, and by God, I wasn't about to stop now. If one of my plans worked out and I succeeded in offing myself, it would take the undertaker all day to get the smile off my face. Bless her heart, she died tragically and much too young, but she had been *such* a cheerful, happy person. I'd take my secret misery to the grave with me, and no one would ever have to know.

I don't know at what point I had lost myself. What had happened to the girl I used to be, the dreamy one who wanted to be a writer, who filled her life with the stories in her head? She used to live in her own little world, but it wasn't a lonely one. It was inhabited by the Ugly Duckling and Black Beauty, Nancy Drew and Jo March, Scarlett O'Hara and Rhett Butler, Elizabeth Bennett and Mr. Darby, Cassandra and the Greek gods and goddesses. She was a girl who craved and sought out solitude, because it was the place where she created her own characters, wrote her own dramas and books. As a girl, her audience had been her little sisters, who begged for bedtime stories, and her classmates, who loved the haunted houses and the way the end of a chapter would draw them into another one. I took that little girl I used to be off to college with me, because way before then she had been reading college-age books and was even more obsessed with writing her own stories by then. She was eager to learn more about writing, to read more books, to sit at the feet of writers who had achieved what she wanted more than anything in the world. She even talked me into believing I could be a playwright, for God's sake! I might not be any good at acting, or have a taste for it, but I loved theater and could do the rest to make it happen. One day, if I followed my dream, I would go to Broadway. I'd write plays or design costumes or paint sets— whatever it took—but I would not settle for a dull, boring life. I would be an *artiste*, a fascinating woman who led a busy, productive life of creativity and adventure.

Who can say what happens to any of the dreams of our younger selves? I know I'm not the first woman of my generation to put hers aside for another life, even the kind of life I'd sworn never to lead. I came of age during the awakening of the women's movement, when we believed we could have it all. And maybe we could have, and maybe some of us did. I thought I could, too, at first. I thought I could marry a brilliant young man, a theologian and activist with radical and exciting dreams, and that we could make a difference in the world. We would raise our children differently than the way we were raised. They would come up in a free and creative environment, with a diversity of people and ideas that we never had in our stifling Southern upbringings. While the dynamic young theologian was preaching, bringing the liberating word of God to his congregations, I'd work my miracles with words, as I'd always wanted. He would preach sermons, and I'd create pageants and programs and books that would transform the lives of others. Life was good, and full of possibilities.

Only, it didn't quite happen that way. As it turned out, it was our lives that were changed, his and mine, and not for the best. Placed in a position where we were dependent on the goodwill of those who had placed us there, we caved. If the sermons became too fiery, or hit too close to home too often, an ambitious young preacher would find himself put out to pasture, serving a church no one else wanted, way out in the boondocks. If—God forbid—the preacher's wife offended someone by speaking her mind or not going along with the status quo, there were severe repercussions. I learned many things during my tenure as a preacher's wife, but one hit home and stuck. It was exactly what my mama had been trying to tell me all my rebellious little life. To make it in this world, to get what you want from it, you have to be a people pleaser. According to my mama, if I would only be what I was raised to be—a sweet, compliant young lady—then everyone would love me to pieces. But if I were to keep swimming against the current, I would see where *that* got me. I couldn't say I wasn't warned.

My mama turned out to be right. As long as I didn't make any waves, I got along with everyone and helped the preacher-man build a successful career. I learned to care, and care a lot, about our self-image and how we were perceived. Gradually, over time, what other people thought about me became a whole lot more important than what I thought about myself. And I liked myself, right? I was being a good girl. Sandra King had been raised to be a *sweet* girl. I was doing good deeds, and making my mama proud. And I could still do my writing, if and when I had time. The church could always use another devotional for the Advent season or a good, heartwarming pageant for the youth department to perform at Easter. Everyone knew the preacher's wife was good at writing things like that. And bless her heart, she was certainly eager to please. All you had to do was ask her, and she'd do it with a big, sweet smile.

It eroded over time, of course, as those kinds of soul-searing things always will. Somewhere during this period, I lost not only myself but God as well. I'd always been a spiritual person, drawn to the mystic and the spiritual world in whatever form it took. At different points in my life, I'd toyed with Buddhism and Hinduism, but found more meaning in the comfortable fit of the familiar, the timeless and beautiful rituals of a community of believers. Even that lost meaning, though, as the image became more important than the imagery. It no longer mattered to me what I believed. The only thing that mattered was making sure no one suspected how lost I was, how empty inside. The persona I had created to cover up my true self had become the only me I knew anymore. A spiritual connection wasn't possible because there was nothing inside me to connect with.

Looking back, I'm not sure I can identify the turning point, the exact moment I knew I could no longer be the *me* I'd become, the depressed, suicidal person who still clung desperately to a self-image that was becoming less valid every day. I do know that for any new life to burst into bloom, something has to die. I had to kill her off, that phony non-person I had created to please others. And I did it the only way I knew, with the only resource that had ever given my inner life any true meaning. I closed the door and started to write. This time, I wasn't writing devotionals or mission studies or Christmas pageants; I was writing my way out of a life that had stifled and imprisoned me. I wrote about my despair, my desperation, my lost identity. Word by word, line by line, I sought to reconnect with myself. No longer did I write to please or impress others—on the contrary, I had no intention of sharing what I was writing with anyone. I hid away and wrote feverishly, disconnected from everyone and everything. Alarmed, the preacher-man suggested I get back to my church work, back to him, back to my family. The congregation had noticed, and were talking about me. What would everyone *think*? At one time, I would have meekly complied, hurriedly putting away my silly little writings as I put my false face back on, then scurried out to meet the world with a big smile firmly in place.

Except this time I couldn't do it anymore. Instead, I stayed put and wrote about a woman's struggles to fit into the mold she had created to please others. The playwright had written a make-believe role, then stepped in to fill it herself. It wasn't a scorned god who had cursed her and caused her to lose her voice; she had cursed herself by denying her voice, by giving it over to others. Freely and willingly, she had given it away. *I* had given it away.

Little did I know it at the time, but during that feverish, stumbling journey of self-discovery, I was creating the underly-

ing themes of all the books I would write from that point on-
ward. The loss of self, the search for identity, and the ultimate
redemption through art would become the foundation for the
stories I would tell, over and over again. Though I still struggle
with depression and probably always will, I'm finally freed from
the suicidal urges of that time in my life. Instead, I want to live
long enough to tell more stories (even if they will always have the
same themes.) I'm finally freed of that prison of my own creation, the even deadlier urge to please others, to let what others
think of me become more important than what I think of myself.

Freeing the self involves a series of painful processes, as
growth always does. For me, it meant leaving behind my life
with the preacher-man and creating a whole new life for myself.
Occasionally it takes a statement, a bold assertion of self that
others might not approve of, a test of sorts. When I left my old
life behind and struck out on my own, I needed such a step to
break free once and for all, and it fell into my lap.

A few years after leaving my old self behind, I met and married another writer. At that time, I'd sold my second novel and
was faced with a bit of a dilemma. I wasn't going to use my new
surname, but how could I continue to write under my former
husband's name, the one on my first novel? The painful associa-
tions made that impossible. I didn't want a pseudonym; what I
really wanted was a whole new identity. I wanted a new me, and
I knew who I wanted her to be. But...if I went through with it,
went to a lawyer and had my name legally changed, what would
people *think*? My old nemesis raised its ugly head, and I faltered.
Here we go again, I thought with a sigh. But I had to do it, and
for the first time in way too many years, I knew that I didn't give
a jolly good damn what anybody else thought. Appearing before
a judge, I told him I was adding three letters to my first name for
professional reasons, since another writer was also named Sandra
King. (I refrained from telling him that I also knew another per-

son by that name, who had once been such a good, sweet little thing). After being fingerprinted and paying the court cost, I came away as Cassandra King, the name I'll take to my grave. I've never thought of it as a new identity. Instead, I see it as a reclaiming of the voice I'd lost so long ago. The whole world might see Cassandra as a ranting, babbling idiot, or they might not believe a word she says. Doesn't matter to me. I like her, and that's all that matters. She is the stranger who is myself.

My Eudaimonia

Emma French Connolly

Today the years float by like paper boats in a fast-moving stream. I want to slow them down, but I cannot. When he still had his right mind, my father said, "Emma, in five years you won't even know this world." He was right. Five years ago I would not have believed my life would be as it is today.

If I were to divide my life into five-year increments, I would make that same statement standing at any point along that timeline.

For much of my life I believed that the purpose of any education was to turn us out into the world as the persons we were created to be and to remain that person for the rest of our days. I thought education put the *Approved* stamp on our lives and souls. From my earliest years I had an understanding that I was supposed to live a linear life; that's what culture teaches us, that life progresses in a certain order. If we follow our true selves, some of us are destined never to live that linear life. I was in my late fifties when I realized I had a false understanding of my true self. Education may make us proficient in a certain field, but it does not make us into who we *are*.

During my time at Millsaps College, a liberal arts school in Jackson, Mississippi, I was exposed to creative and critical thinking. My professors taught me that to be different is to be normal. Now that I have passed the sixty-six-year marker, I believe that the unique person I was created to be was put into my DNA at my making. I did not begin to discover my true self until I approached the fourth quadrant of my life, and I am still discovering today. I like to think of this present time of my life as my first blooming, not my second, because I feel in my soul that my inner self never fully formed on the bud of my earlier years. I view this present time as my own period of eudaimonia, of human flourishing.

I did not wake up one morning and make a decision to flourish, to become. This "becoming" is a process of my total experiences, not just a single event. I believe we are all born as creative beings, but somewhere along the way, for some of us, that creative energy is pushed down or smothered away. We must reach deep into the center of ourselves to find the creative energy that was stifled or stilled, and bring forth an image, a color, a beautiful garment, or a string of words. I do this by writing, painting, sewing, and other means of self-expression. I teach others to find their creative energy.

I sit here in my little shop on Magazine Street in New Orleans, Louisiana, and meet the most interesting people every day. Some, like me, have recently made this city their home and are looking for like-minded creatives. Some are empty-nesters ready to begin to learn new things. Some are moving through all manner of life transitions and need a new craft—knitting, sewing, weaving, painting—to help pull them into their new life of creative energy.

When I assist someone in learning to create, they must be present to the task at hand. By being present, they learn to play again. We converse and I learn about them as they learn about me. Locals embrace me as a kindred spirit. Tourists find my shop through social media or just walking down the street, and they always have a story to tell. Mothers of young girls remember their own reluctance to learn to sew and now bring in their daughters for sewing lessons. I nurture these children as though my own, passing on the knowledge and patience that I learned on the knees of my own grandparents.

I've been stitching since I was seven years old. Both of my grandmothers were sewists and influenced me to be creative. My first experience with a sewing machine was on my paternal grandmother's cabinet model Singer treadle machine. This "green machine" required no electricity, just foot power. My grandmother gave me the machine when she could no longer see well enough to thread a needle. I made my clothes throughout my high school years on that old treadle sewing machine. I loved the look of the machine—the polished wood, the golden labels on the black machine, and the leather belt that turned the wheel as I worked the treadle back and forth.

When I married and had children I made all their clothes. I also made bedspreads, shower curtains, and drapes for all the windows in our homes. But a series of events occurred as I entered the second quadrant of my life that put the brakes on my creativity. I experienced what I came to call my twenty years in the dessert. My marriage began to fail and my creative spirit failed with it. Of necessity, along with a bit of denial of self, I spent those years focusing on my children and just surviving. Creativity had to be put on hold.

When my troubled marriage ended, my daughters' emotions were muddled, my son was addicted to crack, and I was as damaged as a crushed wildflower underfoot. I began the long, slow process of healing. I spent my time in Al-anon meetings and self-help groups, trying to find my true self because I had no idea who I was anymore—if ever I had known my true self. As I continued the process of living I experienced financial crisis after crisis, worked three jobs, and approached physical exhaustion like a whirling dervish.

I was angry, depressed, confused, and hurt. My little brother died. My daughter-in-law died while my son and his family lived with me. Next, my mother and father died. I trudged ahead in survival mode.

As a result of this whirl of grief, crisis, and work, my immune system was compromised, and in 1996 I came down with a strain of West Nile Virus. I had meningitis and encephalitis at the same time. My brain and its lining were infected with this virus and I did not know who I was. I could not remember my name, where I lived, or my children. Parts of my life were gone from my memory. Doctors told my sister that I would be severely disabled and would need home health care. I had to relearn to walk, read, and drive a car. After many months of rehabilitation, I was able to resume a somewhat normal life. I saw my miraculous life through a new lens. I realized such practices as working to exhaustion could not lead to a happy life. Today I am relatively healthy, with no recurring effects of that disease except for occasional cognitive issues, normal for my age anyway.

After recovering from this illness I learned that my great-aunt Neill James had died at her home in Ajijic, Mexico. Aunt Neill was my heroine since I was a little girl. A writer, she was born in Gore Springs, Mississippi, in 1885 and wrote essays and travel books published by Charles C. Scribner Sons. Her editor was Maxwell Perkins, famous literary agent for Ernest Hemingway, F. Scott Fitzgerald, Thomas Wolfe, Marjorie Kinnan Rawlings, and other fine writers. Neill influenced my worldview that women can do anything. She traveled the world and cavorted with Amelia Earhart and notorious entertainers at a time when women of the South did not do such things. Contrary to the desires of the local authorities, she opened a library and art school for local Ajijic children and became famous around her Lake Chapala community. In 2000, I made a pilgrimage to her home and grave in Ajijic, where I felt her presence. I felt her bony fingers poking my shoulder as she said, "You can do anything." She taught me the meaning of moxie. She taught me courage.

I was a single mother for fourteen years before I met my husband Robert. He became instant father and grandfather and has been my cheerleader. He encouraged me to pursue what I felt was a call to the Episcopal diaconate. I was ordained in 2005 and served two churches with my knowledge and skills in pastoral care, family systems, and outreach.

Working with those who were ill, divorcing, hurting, or dying, I learned that I was helping them heal as I myself was healing. Self-expression through the creative arts is a language anyone can understand. In my style of ministry, we did creative writing, hand embroidery, sketching, painting, and hand sewing. I started a nonprofit creative writing program in Memphis, Tennessee, called WriteMemphis, where I engaged volunteers to work with and improve the literacy skills of inner-city youth. As these young people wrote about their home lives, their neighborhoods, their families, they sometimes were able to see the events in their lives as separate from the individuals they really were. Just as with those who were ill and hurting, their true selves were revealed to them through their writing. Creativity heals a hurting soul.

During my years serving as a Parish Deacon in the Episcopal Church, I found solace and healing in my own creativity, and I encouraged others to pursue writing, embroidery, drawing—anything that would bring their emotions outside on the page, on a canvas or on a piece of wool felt. Creativity brings change. This truth came home to me every day as I went about my pastoral work with folks in my care, from the indigent to the affluent.

My home life is filled with writing, painting, sewing, creating. My husband asked me one day as I was sewing something, "What would you do if you did not have to worry about money or the house or the yard or the dogs?" "I would do this," I answered. I had found my bliss. Creativity. Generativity. Empowerment of others.

Although we continued to live and work in Memphis, through our trips to New Orleans (where my father was from, and Robert had lived there too), we decided to retire to New Orleans in 2016. We had spent many weeks there over the years, and one of my daughters had moved there with her family.

On a balmy October New Orleans morning in 2014, my daughter and I had breakfast at a popular French bakery on Magazine Street. Afterwards, we walked around the corner and saw a cute little yellow shotgun house with a small black sign out front that read, *For Lease: Commercial.* An idea bloomed immediately. Within a week I had formulated a business plan, turned sixty-five years old, and had the audacity to sign a two-year lease. I also quit my job in Memphis.

I was uncertain whether I was brave, foolish, or both. I summoned Neill's courage. I am usually a very cautious person who considers all sides of an issue before making decisions. As I age, I find myself more courageous. I do know that when courage arises within me, my creativity is born anew. Sure, there are voices inside my head that say, "You can't succeed at this, you can't afford this, it's too much of a risk." With my husband Robert's encouragement, I did it anyway. We took our retirement savings and invested in our new creativity business here on Magazine Street.

In the first and second quadrants of my life, like most young women of my generation, I tried my best to live according to what I believed were society's norms. Getting married was the goal as the proof that you were worthy. The appearance of your home made you worthy. How the magazines were spread on the coffee table made you worthy. After eighteen years of marriage to my first husband, I found that my worth depended on getting out of an abusive situation. Growing up is a long, slow process. I believe I began to grow up when I reached midlife. I am still maturing.

I've given up my childish trait of perfectionism and listening to my inner critics. I still have spirited debates with my inner saboteurs. *It's too pricey. You have no business doing this at your age! Who do you think you are? Most new businesses fail!* But those voices are much quieter these days.

Why does every creative person I know have an inner critic on the job? No matter if we write, sew, paint, or sculpt, that tiny tyrant tries to be in charge. Mercifully, as I have grown older, that voice has become smaller and smaller. Today it is a mere leaf falling out of place. The analysis of my Myers Briggs testing describes me as "a new puppy, always into something new." That's me. I write, edit, sew, paint, design, and embroider, because there is always something that needs making. This is my passion, for myself and for others. This is what I bring to my new shop, Uptown Needle and Craftworks at 4610 Magazine Street.

My new store is a place for makers who love textiles, embroidery, yarn, and embellishment. We are three businesses in one: consignment and vintage resale; fabric, trim, and yarn store; and a teaching/making space. The shop opened in January 2015 with a mission to empower people of all ages to sew, knit, write, craft, invent, make, and create to their heart's desire. I have wanted to do this for thirty years. Now it is a reality.

John Westerhoff's view of conversion is that it is "a continuous and lifelong process, and…proceeds layer by layer, relationship by relationship, here a little, there a little—until the whole personality, intellect, feeling and will have been recreated by God" (from *The Spiritual Life*). Although he was writing of conversion to Christianity, I believe his statement can apply to our conversion into co-creators with God as we express our true selves. Art comes from that deep place within, our true self.

When we give it some attention, we gather up our courage and we can create something new by being present to the process. I believe in this manner anyone can be converted.

Until Robert retires in summer 2016 and moves to New Orleans full time, I live in a small bedroom at the back of the shop. I have learned to enjoy my minimalist life of using a microwave and dorm fridge, and since there's no room to save everything, I am much more apt to recycle things away—unnecessary emotions along with the junk mail.

Every day I meet new customers who are in a life of transition. Folk such as Lucinda visit every week and take nearly every class I offer. Her husband has a traumatic brain injury and she is healing herself. Michael is another visitor who lives on the street. He stops in every week just to say hello and asks for two quarters to put in the slot machines at the bar in the next block.

Across and down the street is the Buddha Belly Bar and Laundromat. I do my laundry every couple of weeks and have been inspired by the characters that move through there. In my journals I have notes on *Tales from the Buddha Belly*. Characters like Charlie Bob, who lost his foot to an illness and plays a mean guitar to the beat of the washing machine agitation. Or Oretha, who sings like an angel as she removes her clothes from the dryer.

My goals today are to nourish individuals with the grace, gift, and joy of community through being together in collaboration, creativity, and celebration. In my life, I have experienced that some of us cannot bear to be happy, to create something ourselves. Rejection has left us with anger and pain that is sometimes too much to bear. However, sometimes with just a bit of acknowledgment of that pain, we can fully join the celebration of a life of living into our true self.

I've also realized that since I stepped out of my professional clergy role, I am able to create connections and friendships that I otherwise would not have the opportunity to experience.

So what am I now? What label should I wear? I've never liked labels. I refuse to wear one now because labels cut off conversations. My life today is one of participating in community through creativity and collaboration. There are two stools next to my cutting table in the shop. Most days they are occupied as locals and tourists tell me stories about their first attempt to sew or write or whatever creative outlet they have pursued. I love for customers to linger and tell me their experiences. I love for someone to come in and need a button sewn on a jacket. I give them a needle and thread and show them how to do it. I believe this is how to elevate the humble thread to an art form by participating in the act of creation in community.

In my new life I wish to teach others not only *how* to create things but *why*. To show others that they can escape, even momentarily, from the ruthlessness of our often hostile world. I am convinced that we all have glimpses—perhaps from a friend, a dream, or a phrase—of our hidden creative forces that lie dormant. Giving your creativity freedom to grow is enormously rewarding, enriching, and fulfilling. I'm a witness to that truth.

There are many other people doing big important things. I intend to be here in my little shop on Magazine Street, in a mostly blissful life, encouraging others to recognize that creativity is the response to a call—a call from our deepest selves, the part that has no voice but speaks to us and to the world in everything we make, everything we write. That is also a big important thing. Someone once said, "Creativity is our soul's echo." Sounds blissful to me, here in my new life.

I love what Joseph Campbell said about having a "bliss station":

You must have a room, or a certain hour or so a day, where you don't know what was in the newspapers that morning, you don't know who your friends are, you don't know what you owe anybody, you don't know what anybody owes to you. This is a place where you can simply experience and bring forth what you are and what you might be. This is the place of creative incubation. At first you may find that nothing happens there. But if you have a sacred place and use it, something eventually will happen. (http://www.jcf.org)

I have lived a nonlinear life. Thinking back on my early beliefs that a linear life was a necessary path to happiness, I have found the opposite to be true. I want to proclaim that for many, taking a zigzagging path through life is what we are meant to do. Creativity is not just about making art, knitting a sweater, sewing a dress, or writing a book. Creativity is about finding your own eudaimonia. It's about making a life.

The Second Half

Jennifer Horne

I never wanted to be anything but a writer.

Except for when I was fourteen or fifteen and never missed a Jacques Cousteau special, thrilled to the uplift of John Denver's "Calypso," imagined myself inside the pages of Madeleine L'Engle's *The Arm of the Starfish*, and thought I should be a marine biologist. I fell in love with dolphins the way other girls fell in love with horses. Then I dissected my first starfish in high school biology class, almost threw up, couldn't even look at tuna fish sandwiches for a year, and decided maybe being a biologist wasn't for me. The dream was, mostly, a story I had told myself about dolphins. I let go of studying dolphins but kept telling stories.

∽

This essay begins when I was thirty-five. My mother had died a year before, one week before my thirty-fourth birthday, and her illness had exhausted us so much that my sister and I were slow to clear out her things, slow to do the necessary paperwork, slow, even, to erect her headstone. The summer I turned thirty-five we'd decided to work on her office—she was a writer and workshop leader—and I knelt on the soft carpet next to her file cabinets and pulled one open, the overloaded drawer scraping on its rails. Warranties, bank statements, receipts for things she'd ordered from catalogs, handouts on writing exercises, and then a fat file of mostly form letters from journals and book publishers she'd submitted her work to, all the rejections she'd accumulated over the years. I'd known of her publications in local newspapers and statewide anthologies. I hadn't known she'd sent her work farther afield, and had it sent back.

I don't have the rejection letters anymore, can't find them in the big blue plastic storage tubs of her papers, so after I read through them I must have thrown them out, done what she could not or would not do. I wanted to ask her why she'd saved them: for inspiration, a spur to do better, so that she could have a celebratory bonfire when she did finally get those acceptances, or as proof of trying, a record, at least, of taking herself and her work seriously? Physically present or not, those letters sat like a weight on my chest. So much trying and not succeeding. Did she call it failure? What if I, as a writer, ended up only with a file full of rejection letters? I hoped that the writing, her pleasure in seeking meaning and calling up images, had been satisfaction enough. I didn't know whether it would be enough for me.

Near the end of her life, we stood in her living room near the front door of her house out in the country and she almost didn't say but then did, "I wonder what my life would have been like if I had devoted myself to writing," and I, desperate to salvage meaning, desperate for her life and choices and family to have mattered, and desperate not to hear the loss and regret implied in that statement, said, "Your life is your art." She smiled and was pleased with the statement—"That should be my epitaph"—but we didn't talk about death and we also didn't talk anymore about writing.

(When we did finally get her headstone, we chose lines from a poem she loved by Richard Wilbur, "The Milkweed": "What power had I / Before I learned to yield? / Shatter me, great wind, / I shall embrace the field." But—with apologies to Mr. Wilbur, and with trepidation that the Academy of American Poets police force may show up at my door—"shatter" just sounded too harsh at the time, so we changed it to "Scatter me, great wind." It's etched in stone and can't be changed now.)

To me, she was a writer, a poet, always, as well as my mother, but to her there was another, unlived life that involved more writing, less dutifulness and attendance upon societal expectations, not, as she put it, "imprisoned by self-inflicted 'shoulds'; caught in a comparison trap of measurable accomplishments."

Here's a tip: don't, a year after your writer mother dies, go through her papers and discover the rejection slips she saved over the years, files full of them. You may find, as leaves fall on the yard in your own house out in the country, that raking them wearies you into roboticism, no matter how glorious the fall day, how blue the sky. You figure yourself as Sisyphus, the ever-falling leaves your stone, and no matter how many leaves you rake—perhaps I mean to say, no matter how many poems you send out—you can't make any headway.

It soothed me in those days to watch *Martha Stewart Living* at 11:00 a.m. each morning, before or after I taught, depending on the day's teaching schedule. Martha Stewart was living in a way that seemed orderly, explainable, and beautiful. Beauty and order are often what get me through, and she was my Saint of Beauty and Order there for one sad fall.

✍

Or maybe this essay begins when I was eight, winning a prize in the Arkansas Poets Roundtable Poetry Day competitions in a children's category. It was a tennis racquet—how astonishing that I could win a tennis racquet for writing a poem!—and I loved writing poems and I loved hitting tennis balls down at the Cammack Village courts with my mother, who was on her college tennis team and still had a strong forehand and great legs. She was my first reader, and even when I grew up and moved away we called each other with "good lines," relishing the just-right phrase, though I learned later that there were poems she did not ever share, the specifically personal ones about the two toughest and most popular subjects for poets, love and death. Like the one titled "Alien" that describes being on a convention tour bus up in Philadelphia and talking with a woman from Puerto Rico who told of looking forward to visiting her family in New York City. It ends, "That night, I cried. / My sister had died. / Only families speak the same language." She only ever spoke in positive terms of her older sister, how beautiful, how artistically talented, how funny she was. She faced the sadness in her poems but protected us, her daughters, from it. In a prose piece in which she described being saved, at the age of two, from a burning motorcycle that crashed in the front yard of her family's home, she wrote, "I don't think I remember all this because of re-telling. Our family operated on the principle that bad things should be forgotten quickly. I remember."

She always wrote poems, but in her late forties or early fifties she put together a poetry collection titled *The Second Half*, with many of the poems in the voices of female characters, perhaps using personae for things she might not want to say in her own voice, publicly. One of my favorites is titled "Shells."

Shells

I need no talk
With friends who know me well.
I need the feel of sea,
The space of skies.
I need to look at stars,
And look, and look,
Until their light comes back
Into my eyes.

To lie, by timeless day,
On sun-soaked sand,
Not knowing what can end
And what begin.
This is my year to be aware of shells:
Not knowing
If I'm going
Out or in.

I always wrote poems, too, and some stories. In college I took visiting poet Denise Levertov's creative writing workshop and then continued with an English professor/poet with the wonderful name of Ashby Bland Crowder. Ideally—naively—I had wanted to be Keats without the tuberculosis, savoring early poetic success and looking forward to a lifetime of publication in *The New Yorker*, *Poetry*, and the *Paris Review*. Entering a Master of Fine Arts in Creative Writing Program when I was twenty-six only enhanced my expectation of being launched onto the poetry scene upon graduation at age thirty. I thought I'd make headway steadily, build my list of publications, begin publishing books, and establish myself in the decade after graduation. Surely, now that I had been stamped "Poet," my inner identity would be matched by outward acceptance and appearance.

This essay could surely begin in what I called, to myself, "the year before forty," when I quit my full-time job to work part-time and write, determined to have publishing success before I hit my fifth decade. Although I had published some poems here and there, I felt stuck. Despite sending poetry manuscripts to dozens of contests and spending hundreds of dollars on entry fees, I had managed only one semi-finalist slot. Maybe, like marine biology, writing wasn't for me either, except perhaps as a private hobby. I tried this position out, but it only made me cranky and difficult to live with, slimily envious of others' first books. I was simultaneously frustrated with my lack of progress and angry with myself for caring so much. It wasn't fair, somehow: hadn't I done everything right, made all A's in my classes, filled out all the forms correctly? One more contest, I thought: the Yale Series of Younger Poets Prize is awarded annually to a poet under forty, and for the final time I entered a manuscript in the contest. I did not win. There is no Yale Series of Older Poets Prize.

There are certain truths in life. One is that if you decide to run out to Wendy's to get a salad because your kitchen is being painted, your car is much more likely to break down if you have been working in your house in grubby clothes and are sweaty, dirty-haired, un-made-up, and famished than if you are ready for your close-up. As you sit by the side of a country road in ninety-five-degree heat, eating stale saltines from the glove box, having primped the best you could by brushing your hair and pulling out your emergency stash of face powder so that you look something like Southern-presentable when Wayne's Wrecker arrives, you ponder how life's little unpredictable moments will confound your attempts to control how the world sees you.

Another truth is that if you think you know exactly how your success will arrive and in what form, you will very likely be disappointed.

My part-time job morphed into a full-time job, and before I knew it I had a position with a great deal of responsibility but not much creativity. Hungry for a creative project that could be managed in parts rather than with great hunks of time, I got the idea for an anthology of poems about gardening, which became an anthology of poems about both gardening and farming, which turned out to be a kind of agricultural history in poems of the rural and post-rural South. *Working the Dirt: An Anthology of Southern Poets* was my first book.

More books followed, books I wrote and books I edited. Although I hope to do even more and even better with my writing, I feel as if I've finally gotten there (wherever *there* is). A book of short stories that's done fairly well and taken me all over the Southeast to conferences and book festivals, a book of poems accepted by an Irish publisher—these feel real to me. My insides and my outsides match: I *am* a writer, and my life looks like the life of a writer. The arc of this narrative, then, looks like struggle and eventual success—but it is also the story of facing what looked like failure, a future without tennis racquets or any other prizes, and deciding I would still write because I needed to, because the world feeds my senses which feed my brain which then, in T. S. Eliot's words, engages in "mixing memory and desire," not cruelly but productively, taking remembered experience and infusing it with feeling. (I know those words from Eliot because I fell in love with his work as an undergraduate. When the Administration Building on campus burned one cold night, I painted words from the "East Coker" section of *The Four Quartets* on a piece of wood and placed it, anonymously, by the ruins: "In my beginning is my end. In succession / Houses rise and fall, crumble, are extended, / Are removed, destroyed, restored, or in their place / Is an open field, or a factory, or a by-pass. / Old stone to new building, old timber to new fires, / Old fires to ashes, and ashes to the earth….")

Art gets us through, I've always believed, I've always found. In "One Art," a marvelous villanelle that insistently repeats what we all know not to be true, Elizabeth Bishop writes that "the art of losing isn't hard to master": "It's evident / the art of losing's not too hard to master / though it may look like (*Write* it!) like disaster." If you can write it, you can stand it. I imagine that many others have, like me, taken comfort in Bishop's face-into-the-wind bravado.

In an untitled piece that begins, "I do not know enough to make the decision that faces me," my mother wrote of calling a friend, "long distance" as we said then, who listened, and then told her to "sit down and start writing." Her friend said to "Write for days. Write whatever comes to mind of your life. Write the bad as well as the good."

I'm fifty-five now. My mother died at fifty-nine, more than twenty years ago. I knew, then, that she was too young, but I really meant "too young to leave me." I didn't feel ready, at thirty-four, to be without her. Sitting here, however, as late-autumn sun warms my writing room and a breeze stirs the chimes, I ponder where my next thirty years (should I live to be eighty-five) might take me, and I know what a thief her early death was, denying her a full second half. Still, I take comfort knowing she was doing the work she needed to do, coming into a selfhood that did not fit with her childhood programming of "being good," and "seeking praise in grown-up ways." She wrote, became a licensed massage therapist, swam with dolphins, and dubbed herself a "Sufi-Episcopalian," claiming the old *and* the new. I can't say that I believe, for sure, that there was a chapter for her beyond this life's, but I can't say I *dis*believe it, either.

The summer before last, I decided to take on a reclamation project of sorts, typing my mother's poems, hundreds of them, onto the computer from her typed or handwritten versions. I was afraid that it would be painful, but I wanted to save them for sharing with friends and family, possibly in a book, now that self-publishing has become so much easier. It was, instead, the opposite of painful: deeply satisfying and rewarding, opening up

215

a new understanding of her as a writer and a person. It connected me with my mother in an almost physical way as I typed the words she had written, as though my hands were sitting on top of hers, learning chords on the grand piano she'd refinished herself, playing her favorite songs as dusk began to fall over our woods, the heavy curtains not yet closed. I saw her in uncertainty: "My maps lead nowhere. / I will let life show me." She was often contemplative, as in the short poem "Communion": "Eyes look down / Souls look up." She was loving and observant in a poem for my sister—"Blue are Mary's eyes / Depths like the great arch of sky / In them is beauty"—and maternally protective of me in these lines: "What do you do with a feeling child? / Face lit by sun and rainbows? / Take joy in her delight / ...What do you do with a feeling child / Whose face is hopeless winter rain / On seeing fairness flouted..."

To a friend on her birthday she wrote, "Good things take time: / Knit sweaters, fine tucked camisoles, / and friendship; / Bread to rise, / Wine to age; All things in urgent need of healing / Seeds of morning glory vine / to sprout and climb." Of a possible new love, after my parents' divorce: "I connected with you / Because we connect. / I do not spend time / Wishing / That I had been coy."

My current writing project is a long-researched, much-pondered "personal biography" of a woman named Sara Mayfield who grew up in Tuscaloosa and Montgomery, Alabama, was a childhood friend of Zelda Sayre Fitzgerald, studied in London, ran her family's farm in the Black Belt, worked as a print and radio journalist, and spent seventeen years as a patient in the state mental hospital, Bryce, adjacent to the UA campus, after being involuntarily committed by her mother. She was diagnosed with "paranoid condition" but became well enough to live on her own, and it was after her release from the hospital in 1965, at the age of fifty-six, that she published her three books, *Exiles from*

Paradise (1971), on the Fitzgeralds; *The Constant Circle* (1969), a biography of H. L. Mencken; and a historical novel, *Mona Lisa* (1974). She was interviewed for the *Tuscaloosa News*, UA's *Crimson White*, and the *Anniston (Ala.) Star*, won the 1969 Alabama Library Association Award for her book on Mencken, was a featured speaker at her undergraduate alma mater Goucher College, traveled abroad, and continued to keep up a voluminous and energetic correspondence with friends and family and an active social life, mentoring younger writers, until her death.

I figured out somewhere along the way that the Mayfield project was tied in with my own questions about the women of my family as artists and writers, investigating how they balanced traditional roles and expectations with the need to do art—and how conforming to those roles conflicted with the sometimes chaotic and irregular demands of creative thinking. One of the great dangers, it seems to me, is becoming "eccentric." As a noun, "eccentric" is so often preceded by the adjective "harmless." To be labeled eccentric and to accept that label is to be neutralized, safely categorized as "out of the center," as the word's etymology suggests—someone easily ignored. I seek a more dangerous centrality, a normalcy of inclusion. In writing of Sara Mayfield, I have had to decide to do the book my way rather than the "right" way, perhaps confounding standard expectations of what a biography should be.

I'm writing my way into this book, writing my way into my own discoveries about the past and what I need to understand in order to live fully in the present. I sit in the floral-upholstered chair my mother bought from Ethan Allen, the one she said she "planned to grow old in," and ponder what comes next, and next after that.

Liturgy

Natasha Trethewey

from Beyond Katrina: A Meditation on the
Mississippi Gulf Coast

People carry with them the blueprints of memory for a place. It
is not uncommon to hear directions given in terms of landmarks
that are no longer there: "turn right at the corner where the fruit
stand used to be," or "across the street from the lot where Miss
Mary used to live." Aesha tells me there are no recognizable
landmarks along the coast anymore, and I see this too as I drive
down the beach. No way to get your bearings. No way to feel at
home, familiar with the land and cityscape. In time, the landmarks of destruction and rebuilding will overlap and intersect the
memory of what was there—narrative and metanarrative—the
pentimento of the former landscape shown only through the
memories of the people who carry it with them. With fewer people in the area who remember the pre-Katrina landscape and
culture, there's a much greater chance that it will be forgotten.
Too, the memory of such events requires the collective efforts of
a people—each citizen contributing to the narrative—so that a
fuller version of the story can be told. In that way, one hope we
can have for the future, beyond the necessities with which we
must concern ourselves—environmentally sound rebuilding, fair
and equal recovery—is the continuity of culture and heritage fos-
tered by ongoing change and honest, inclusive remembrance of
the past.

Rituals of commemoration serve to unite communities
around collective memory, and at the second anniversary of the

storm people gathered to remember—some at church or community centers, others at locations that held more private significance. Personal recollections are equally integral to the larger story. Johnny, a card dealer at one of the casinos—a friend of my brother's who did not leave—says that he stayed home to watch the national news. He wanted to see how the anniversary and the recovery were being understood outside the region. Then he took a kind of memorial drive—"just riding down the beach," he said, "trying to find places I used to go." Aesha marked the anniversary by donating blood. When I ask them both about what they do year round to keep the memory of the storm and its aftermath, and about whether there is a danger in forgetting, Johnny takes the diplomatic approach: "You have to learn from history," he says. Shaking her head, Aesha is more adamant about the memory of the storm. "There is no forgetting," she says. "You can't forget—you won't." In her words, an imperative, a command.

ᵔᕲ

Some time ago—before the storm—my grandmother and I were shopping in Gulfport, and we met a friend of hers shopping with her granddaughter too. The woman introduced the girl to us by her nickname, then quickly added the child's given name. My grandmother, a proud woman—not to be outdone—replied, "Well, Tasha's name is really *Nostalgia*," drawing the syllables out to make the name seem more exotic. I was embarrassed and immediately corrected her, not anticipating that the guilt I'd feel later could be worse than my initial chagrin. Perhaps she was trying to say Natalya, the formal version, in Russian, to which Natasha is the diminutive. At both names' Latin root: the idea of nativity, of the birthday of Christ. They share a prefix with words like *natal*, *national*, and *native*. "I write what is given me to write," Phil Levine has said. I've been given to thinking that it's my national duty, my native duty, to keep the memory of my Gulf Coast as talisman against the uncertain future. But my grandmother's misnomer is compelling too; she was on to something when she called me out with it.

I think of Hegel again: "When we turn to survey the past, the *first* thing we see is nothing but ruins." The first thing we see. The fears for the future, expressed by the people I spoke with on the coast, are driven by the very real landscape of ruin and by environmental and economic realities associated with development, but they are driven by nostalgia too. When we begin to imagine a future in which the places of our past no longer exist, we see *ruin*. Perhaps this is nowhere most evident than in my own relationship to the memory of my home.

Everywhere I go during my journey, I feel the urge to weep not only for the residents of the coast but also for my former self: the destroyed public library is *me* as a girl, sitting on the floor, reading between the stacks; empty, debris-strewn downtown Gulfport is *me* at the Woolworth's lunch counter—early 1970s—with my grandmother; is *me* listening to the sounds of shoes striking the polished tile floor of Hancock Bank, holding my grandmother's hand, waiting for candy from the teller behind her wicket; *me* riding the elevator of the J. M. Salloum Building—the same elevator my grandmother operated in the thirties; *me* waiting in line at the Rialto movie theater—gone for more years now than I can remember—where my mother also stood in line at the back door for the peanut gallery, the black section where my grandmother, still a girl, went on days designated colored only, clutching the coins she earned selling crabs; is *me* staring at my reflection in the glass at J. C. Penney's as my mother calls, again and again, my name. I hear it distantly, as through water of memory too—Katrina, Camille. Perhaps this is why we name our storms.

∾

When Camille hit in 1969, I was three years old. Across the street from my grandmother's house, the storm tore the roof off the Mount Olive Baptist Church. A religious woman, my grandmother believed the Lord had spared her home—a former shotgun to which more rooms had been added—and damaged, instead, the large red-brick church and many of the things inside, thus compelling her to more devotion. During renovation the church got a new interior: deep red carpet and red velvet draperies for the baptismal font—made by my grandmother, her liturgy to God's House. In went a new organ and a marble altar bearing the words *Do This In Remembrance Of Me.* As a child I was frightened by these words, the object—a long rectangle, like a casket—upon which they were inscribed; I believed quite literally that the marble box held a body. Such is the power of monumental objects to hold within them the weight of remembrance.

And yet I spent so little time in the church when I was growing up that I'm surprised now that so much of my thinking comes to me in the language of ceremony. But then, when I look up the word *liturgy*, I find that in the original Greek it means, simply, *one's public duty, service to the state undertaken by a citizen.*

I am not a religious woman. This is my liturgy to the Mississippi Gulf Coast:

Liturgy

To the security guard staring at the Gulf
thinking of bodies washed away from the coast,
    plugging her ears
against the bells and sirens—sound of alarm—
    the gaming floor
on the coast;

To Billy Scarpetta, waiting tables on the coast,
    staring at the Gulf
thinking of water rising, thinking of New Orleans,
    thinking of cleansing
the coast;

To the woman dreaming of returning to the coast,
    thinking of water rising,
her daughter's grave, my mother's grave—underwater—
    on the coast;

To Miss Mary, somewhere;

To the displaced, living in trailers along the coast,
    beside the highway,
in vacant lots and open fields; to everyone who stayed
    on the coast,
who came back—or cannot—to the coast;

To those who died on the coast.

This is a memory of the coast: to each his own
recollections, her reclamations, their
restorations, the return of the coast.

This is a time capsule for the coast: words of the people
—*don't forget us*—
the sound of wind, waves, the silence of graves,
the muffled voice of history, bulldozed and buried
under sand poured on the eroding coast,
the concrete slabs of rebuilding the coast.

This is a love letter to the Gulf Coast, a praise song, a dirge, invocation and benediction, a requiem for the Gulf Coast.

This cannot rebuild the coast; it is an indictment,
    a complaint,
my *logos*—argument and discourse—with the coast.

This is my *nostos*—my pilgrimage to the coast, my memory, my reckoning—

native daughter: I am the Gulf Coast.

Nine months after Katrina, I went home for the first time. Driving down Highway 49, after passing my grandmother's house, I went straight to the cemetery where my mother is buried. It was more ragged than usual—the sandy plots overgrown with weeds. The fence around it was still up, so I counted the entrances until I reached the fourth one, which opened onto the gravel road where I knew I'd find her. I searched first for the large, misshapen shrub that had always shown me to her grave, and found it gone. My own negligence had revisited me, and I stood there foolishly, a woman who'd never erected a monument on her mother's grave. I walked in circles, stooping to push back grass and weeds until I found the concrete border that marked the plots of my ancestors. It was nearly overtaken, nearly sunken beneath the dirt and grass. How foolish of me to think of monuments and memory, of inscribing the landscape with narratives of remembrance, as I stood looking at my mother's near-vanished grave in the post-Katrina landscape to which I'd brought my heavy bag of nostalgia. I see now that remembrance is an individual duty as well—a duty native to us as citizens, as daughters and sons. Private liturgy: I vow to put a stone here, emblazoned with her name.

Not far from the cemetery, I wandered the vacant lot where a church had been. Debris still littered the grass. Everywhere, there were pages torn from hymnals, Bibles, psalms pressed into the grass as if they were cemented there. I bent close, trying to read one; to someone driving by along the beach, I must have looked like a woman praying.

Contributors

Jennifer Bradner

Jennifer Bradner is the author of *Letters to Hagar*, a collection of short essays that parallels Hagar as a common saint of the Christian, Jewish, and Muslim heritages while telling the story of modern life filled with ancestral curses. Jen's home is Memphis, where she is active in the interfaith/intercultural community. She teaches entrepreneurialism to art students at the Memphis College of Art and is a happy member of the Pema Karpo Buddhist Community. Jen spent six years as CFO then Executive Director of Opera Memphis. Most recently, Jen accepted the position of Chief Operating Officer of the Memphis Symphony Orchestra, working closely with the CEO and Board of Trust to create a sustainable business model to address the rapidly changing needs of the classical world.

Julie Cantrell

New York Times and *USA Today* best-selling author Julie Cantrell has served as editor-in-chief of the *Southern Literary Review* and is a recipient of the Mississippi Arts Commission Literary Fellowship. She is the author of two children's books as well as *Into the Free,* which received the Christy Award for Book of the Year (2013) as well as the Mississippi Library Association's Fiction Award. This debut novel also received a rare starred review by Publishers Weekly and was selected as one of five finalists for the University of Mississippi Common Reading Experience 2014. Additionally, it was selected as a best novel of 2013 by LifeWay, *USA TODAY*, and many book clubs. Cantrell's sophomore novel, *When Mountains Move*, is the sequel to her debut. Since its release in September 2013, it has been named a 2013 Best Read by LifeWay, was shortlisted for several awards, and won the 2014 Carol Award for Historical Fiction. Her third novel, *The Feathered Bone*, was released in January 2016. Cantrell lives in Oxford, Mississippi.

Emma French Connolly

Emma Connolly is a writer, artist, and clothing designer for little girls under the label French Boundary. Her award-winning stories include fiction and creative nonfiction, and one of her novel manuscripts was a finalist in Amazon's Great American Novel contest. As founder of WriteMemphis (now a program of Literacy Mid-South), she loves writing with others, especially teens, and facilitated a spiritual writing group for many years. One of her published essays is the story of her own teenage pregnancy and the difficult decision to give up her child for adoption. She is also a deacon in the Episcopal Church and served on the staff of St. John's in Memphis until fall 2014, when she retired from St. John's and moved to New Orleans to open Uptown Needle & Craftworks, a sewing and creative arts studio on Magazine Street.

Susan Cushman (Editor)

Susan Cushman was Co-Director of the 2013 and 2010 Creative Nonfiction Conferences (Oxford, Mississippi) and Director of the 2011 Memphis Creative Nonfiction Workshop (Memphis, Tennessee). She has served as panelist or speaker at book festivals in five states. Cushman's book *Tangles and Plaques: A Mother and Daughter Face Alzheimer's* was published in January 2017. She has ten published essays in various journals and magazines and three in the following anthologies: *Circling Faith: Southern Women on Spirituality* (University of Alabama Press, 2012); *The Shoe Burnin': Stories of Southern Soul* (Rivers Edge Media, Little Rock AR, 2013); and *Dumped: Stories of Women*

Unfriending Women (She Writes Press, February 2015). Her novel *Cherry Bomb* made the short list for the 2011 Faulkner-Wisdom Creative Writing Competition ("Novel-in-Progress" division). She grew up in Mississippi and has lived in Memphis since 1988. Follow her on Facebook and read her blog, "Pen and Palette," at www.susancushman.com.

Beth Ann Fennelly

Beth Ann Fennelly is Professor of English at the University of Mississippi, where she was named the 2011 Outstanding Liberal Arts Teacher of the Year. She's currently serving a four-year term as Mississippi Poet Laureate. She's won grants from the N.E.A., the MS Arts Commission, and United States Artists. Her work has three times been included in *The Best American Poetry* Series. Fennelly has published three full-length poetry books. Her first, *Open House*, won the 2001 *Kenyon Review* Prize and the Great Lakes College Association New Writers Award, and was a Book Sense Top Ten Poetry Pick. Her second book, *Tender Hooks*, and her third, *Unmentionables*, were published by W. W. Norton in 2004 and 2008. She has also published a book of nonfiction, *Great with Child*, in 2006 with Norton. Fennelly writes essays on travel, culture, and design for *Country Living*, *Southern Living*, *AFAR*, *The Oxford American*, and others. *The Tilted World*, the novel she co-authored with her husband, Tom Franklin, was published by HarperCollins in October of 2014, and is an Indie Next, Okra, and LibraryReads selection. They live in Oxford with their three children.

Nina Gaby

Nina Gaby is a writer, visual artist, and psychiatric nurse practitioner living in central Vermont. She has contributed to numerous anthologies and periodicals, both fiction and nonfiction, as well as prose poetry and articles. She is the editor of

Dumped: Stories of Women Unfriending Women, published by She Writes Press in 2015. Most recently her creative nonfiction is appearing in *Entropy Magazine, Kevin MD, Intima: A Journal of Narrative Medicine*, the anthology *Mothering through Darkness*, and the upcoming *How Does That Make You Feel?* Gaby is a finalist in *The Diagram*'s 2016 essay contest, and she has guest blogged on a number of sites including Brevity.com, Intima, ChickLit Central, and infrequently on her own website at www.ninagaby.com. Her sculptural porcelain is in the National Collection of the Renwick at the Smithsonian, and Arizona State University. Gaby's three-dimensional memoir vessels explore transparency/translucency/opacity in mixed media including the written word and have been exhibited in numerous regional gallery exhibits. Her vignette collection, *Overheard: Story/gesture*, is looking for a home as she works on her second collection, *Rules for a Working Life*.

Jessica Handler

Jessica Handler is the author of two books of nonfiction, *Braving the Fire: A Guide to Writing About Grief* and *Invisible Sisters: A Memoir*. *Invisible Sisters* was named one of the "25 Books All Georgians Should Read." Handler's story captures the devastating effects of illness and death on a family and the triumphant account of one woman's enduring journey to step out of the shadow of loss to find herself anew. Her essays and nonfiction features have appeared on NPR, and in *Tin House, Drunken Boat, Full Grown People, Brevity, Newsweek, The Washington Post, More Magazine*, and the anthology *Dumped: Women Unfriending Women*. She earned her MFA in Creative Writing from Queens University of Charlotte (NC) and a BS in Communication from Emerson College in Boston. Featured as one of nine contemporary Southern women writers in *Vanity Fair* magazine, she learned never again to wear couture. She lives in an old house in Atlanta with her husband and more than one cat.

Suzanne Henley

Suzanne Henley taught college-prep and community college English for what felt like forever; held PR/marketing/ development positions with the local public radio and TV affiliate, The Children's Museum of Memphis, and Metropolitan Inter-Faith Association; was a columnist and feature writer for Memphis-area magazines; and was director of development at Memphis College of Art. Since 2000 she's bought, gutted, redesigned and, with her crew, renovated ten early-twentieth-century cottages; created commissions of more than 800 sets of individualized ecumenical prayer beads and of private and corporate wall commissions in fused glass, ancient beads, and copper; worked for a hospice agency training and placing volunteers; and served on community boards. She is the coauthor and illustrator of the cookbook *Sauce for the Goose* and author of *Bead by Bead* (2017).

Jennifer Horne

Raised in Arkansas and a longtime resident of Alabama, Jennifer Horne is a writer, editor, and teacher who explores Southern identity and experience, especially women's, through prose, poetry, fiction, and anthologies and in classrooms and workshops across the South. Her latest book is *Tell the World You're a Wildflower*, a collection of short stories in the voices of Southern women and girls. She is the author of two poetry chapbooks and a poetry collection, *Bottle Tree*, and the editor of *Working the Dirt: An Anthology of Southern Poets*. With Wendy Reed, she co-edited the essay collections *All Out of Faith: Southern Women on Spirituality* and *Circling Faith: Southern Women on Spirituality*. In 2016 her second collection of poems, *Little Wanderer*, was published in Ireland by Salmon Publishing. With Don

Noble, she is editing *Belles' Letters II,* an anthology of short fiction by Alabama women, and she also is at work on a biography of writer Sara Mayfield.

River Jordan

River Jordan began her writing career as a playwright and spent over ten years in the theater both writing and directing. She went on to become a best-selling author. Her work has been most frequently cast in the company of such authors as O'Conner, Faulkner, and Harper Lee. In the fullness of time, Ms. Jordan's spiritual memoir, *Confessions of an American Mystic* (Jericho Books/Hachette), will arrive in bookstores everywhere.

Mary Karr

Mary Karr is an award-winning poet and best-selling memoirist. She is the author of *Lit,* the long-awaited sequel to her critically acclaimed and *New York Times* best-selling memoirs *The Liars' Club* and *Cherry.* Karr added yet another title, songwriter, to her pedigree with the release of *Kin,* Songs by Mary Karr and Rodney Crowell, on Vanguard Records. Produced by Joe Henry, *Kin* marks the first collaboration between the two writers and is Karr's entry into the world of music. A born raconteur, Karr brings to her lectures and talks the same wit, irreverence, joy, and sorrow found in her poetry and prose. She has won prizes from Best American Poetry as well as Pushcart Prizes for both poetry and essays. Her four volumes of poetry are *Sinners Welcome, Viper Rum, The Devil's Tour,* and *Abacus.* She lives in Syracuse, New York, and New York City.

Cassandra King

Cassandra King is the award-winning author of five novels, most recently the critically acclaimed *Moonrise* (2013), her literary homage to *Rebecca* by Daphne du Maurier. *Moonrise* was a

Fall 2013 Okra Pick and a Southern Independent Booksellers Alliance (SIBA) bestseller. Her previous books include *The Same Sweet Girls Guide to Life: Advice from a Failed Southern Belle* (2014), *Queen of Broken Hearts* (2008), *The Same Sweet Girls* (2005), and *Making Waves* (1995, reissued in 2004). She says that the writing of *The Sunday Wife* (2002)—and divorcing her Methodist minister husband—was her salvation. A native of L.A. (Lower Alabama), King currently lives in Beaufort, South Carolina, in the home she shared with her late husband, Pat Conroy.

Anne Lamott

Anne Lamott is the author of seven novels including, *Hard Laughter, Rosie, Joe Jones, Blue Shoe, All New People, Crooked Little Heart,* and *Imperfect Birds.* She has also written several bestselling books of nonfiction, including *Operating Instructions,* an account of life as a single mother during her son's first year, followed by *Some Assembly Required: A Journal of My Son's First Son,* and a writing guide, *Bird by Bird: Some Instructions on Writing and Life.* She has also authored three collections of autobiographical essays on faith: *Traveling Mercies: Some Thoughts on Faith, Plan B: Further Thoughts on Faith,* and *Grace (Eventually): Thoughts on Faith.* In her book of nonfiction, *Help, Thanks, Wow: The Three Essential Prayers,* Ms. Lamott gives us three prayers to assist us in trying times. Her book *Stitches: A Handbook on Meaning, Hope, and Repair* is an honest, funny book about how to make sense of life's chaos. Her newest book of essays is called *Small Victories: Spotting Improbable Moments of Grace* (November 2014). Lamott has been honored with a Guggenheim Fellowship and has taught at UC Davis as well as at writing conferences across the country.

Susan Marquez

Susan Marquez has an intense curiosity to learn and the courage to write that has led her to a career of freelance writing for magazines, newspapers, business journals, and trade publications. After a twenty-one-year career in advertising and marketing, she began writing articles in 2001, with nearly 2,000 published to date. In 2008, Susan began writing daily on her daughter's Caring Bridge, a website for people with serious health issues. Her poignant posts quickly drew a large following of people anxious to learn what was happening with the recovery of her daughter. She'll soon publish a book with lessons learned from those trying times. An empty-nester, Susan is enjoying life with Larry, her husband of thirty-five years, and their two entertaining dogs.

Alexis Paige

Alexis Paige's work appears in multiple journals and anthologies, including *The Pinch*, *New Madrid Journal*, *Fourth Genre*, *The Rumpus*, *Pithead Chapel*, and on Brevity, where she is an assistant editor. Winner of the 2013 New Millennium Writings Nonfiction Prize, she also received two recent Pushcart Prize nominations, and features on *Freshly Pressed* and *Longform*. Twice a top-ten finalist of *Glamour Magazine*'s essay contest, Paige holds an MA in poetry from San Francisco State University and an MFA in nonfiction from the University of Southern Maine. Her essay, "The Right to Remain," published in *The Rumpus*, was named a notable in the *2016 American Best Essays* anthology. Her first book, *Not a Place on Any Map*—a collection of lyric essays that explore the geographical and metaphorical intersections of trauma and dislocation—won the 2016 Vine Leaves Press Vignette Collection Award and was published in December 2016. You can find her online at alexispaigewrites.com.

Ellen Morris Prewitt

Ellen's first book, *Making Crosses: A Creative Connection to God*, was published by Paraclete Press (2009). Her essay "Tetanus, you Understand?" was included in Sue Silverman's *Fearless Confessions: A Writers' Guide to Memoir*. Her work has appeared in *Hotel Amerika*, *Barrelhouse*, *Image*, *Gulf Coast*, *Brevity*, *Fourth Genre*, *Alaska Quarterly Review*, and elsewhere. She was the Peter Taylor Fellow at the Kenyon College Summer Writing Program. A short story received a Special Mention from Pushcart Prize; another was nominated. The stories in her collection *Cain't Do Nothing with Love* have been downloaded worldwide over 30,000 times; the collection won the CIPA EVVY 2014 Award in Audio Book. Her radio commentary received PRNDI recognition from NPR. Her novel-in-progress was a Short List Finalist in the William Faulkner-William Wisdom Competition 2015. She facilitates a weekly writing group of Memphians who have experienced homelessness; she edited the group's book, *Writing Our Way Home: A Group Journey Out of Homelessness* (Triton Press, 2014). For this work, she was named Upstander by Facing History and Ourselves and awarded the Memphis/Shelby County 2015 Homeless Consortium Champion of the Year Award. Ellen practiced law for nineteen years. For six years she worked as a runway model. She splits her time between Memphis and New Orleans.

Wendy Reed

Wendy Reed is an award-winning public TV producer (*Bookmark* and *Discovering Alabama*, for which she received two Emmys) and writer whose books include *An Accidental Memoir: Circling Faith and All Out of* Faith, co-edited with Jennifer Horne. She also teaches in the Honors College at the University of Alabama. Her stories and essays have appeared in various publications, most recently *Belles' Letters I* and *The Shoe Burnin': Stories of Southern Soul.*

Kathy Rhodes

Kathy Rhodes is author of *Remember the Dragonflies: A Memoir of Grief and Healing* and *Pink Butterbeans: Stories From the Heart of a Southern Woman.* Her essay, "An Open Letter," appeared in *The Best Creative Nonfiction, Volume 3* and was singled out for a review in *The New Yorker.* Her essay "The Wedding Hankie" was included in *Chocolate for a Woman's Soul II.* She has served as editor of two anthologies, and her works have been included in seven anthologies. She has served on panels at the Southern Festival of Books in Nashville. Rhodes teaches writing workshops and has presented at state writers' conferences. For eight years she was publisher/editor of the e-zine Muscadine Lines: A Southern Journal, ISSN 1554-8449, which published the works of 361 writers in 38 states and 10 countries. Currently, Rhodes lives in the Nashville area and is senior writer/editor for TurnStyle Writers.

Kim Michele Richardson

Kim Michele Richardson spent over nine years in the care of the Sisters of Charity of Nazareth in her native Kentucky in the 1960s. That grim experience and her subsequent legal action against the nuns were the subjects of her best-selling memoir, *The Unbreakable Child.* Kim Michele resides in the rolling hills of Kentucky where she is a volunteer for Habitat for Humanity and an advocate for the prevention of child abuse and domestic violence. She is also the author of *Liar's Bench,* her first novel. She is a contributor to the *Huffington Post.* Kim Michele's second novel, *God Pretty in the Tobacco Field,* was published in spring 2016.

Sally Palmer Thomason

Sally Palmer Thomason, born and raised in California, attended Occidental College and the International Graduate School of the University of Stockholm. Having lived in Memphis since the mid-1950s, she taught history at St. Mary's Episcopal School and was dean of lifelong learning at Rhodes College, where she developed interdisciplinary programs in the humanities and social sciences. After earning a PhD from The Union Institute and University when she was in her sixties, she taught courses on aging at the Memphis Theological Seminary and has continued to explore the ways culture shapes an individual's beliefs and values in the three books she has written during her "second blooming"—*The Living Spirit of the Crone: Turning Aging Inside Out*, *The Topaz Brooch*, and *Delta Rainbow: The Irrepressible Betty Bobo Pearson*.

Natasha Trethewey

Natasha Trethewey served two terms as the 19th Poet Laureate of the United States (2012–2014). She is the author of four collections of poetry: *Thrall* (2012); *Native Guard* (2006), for which she was awarded the Pulitzer Prize; *Bellocq's Ophelia* (2002); and *Domestic Work* (2000), which was selected by Rita Dove as the winner of the inaugural Cave Canem Poetry Prize for the best first book by an African American poet and won both the 2001 Mississippi Institute of Arts and Letters Book Prize and the 2001 Lillian Smith Award for Poetry. Her book of nonfiction, *Beyond Katrina: A Meditation on the Mississippi Gulf Coast*, was published in 2010. She is the recipient of fellowships from the National Endowment for the Arts, the Guggenheim Foundation, the Rockefeller Foundation, the Beinecke Library at Yale, and the Bunting Fellowship Program of the Radcliffe Institute for Advanced Study at Harvard. At Emory University she is the Robert W. Woodruff Professor of English and Creative

Writing. In 2012 she was named Poet Laureate of the State of Mississippi, and in 2013 she was inducted into the American Academy of Arts and Sciences.

NancyKay Sullivan Wessman

Veteran journalist and public health communications expert NancyKay Wessman writes, edits, reads, and tells stories. Her latest work of creative nonfiction reveals true accounts from first responders to the catastrophic hurricane that targeted Mississippi in 2005. *Katrina, Mississippi: Voices from Ground Zero* celebrates and commemorates their work toward rebuilding the Mississippi Gulf Coast. She also authored, in 2012, a book for parents about lessons learned regarding children's heart health in the forty-year-and-running Bogalusa Heart Study.

Permissions